D1103844

The Environmental Handbook for Property Transfer and Financing

Michael K. Prescott, P.E.
Douglas S. Brossman, Esq.

Library of Congress Cataloging-in-Publication Data

Prescott, Michael K., 1956-
    The environmental handbook for property transfer and financing /
Michael K. Prescott, Douglas S. Brossman.
        p. cm.
    Includes bibliographical references and index.
    ISBN 0-87371-360-5
    1. Liability and environmental damages — United States. 2. Vendors
and purchasers — United States. 3. Environmental law — United States.
I. Brossman, Douglas S.   II. Title.
KF1298.P74   1990
344.73′ 046—dc20
[347.30446]   90-6466
                                                                  CIP

LEWIS PUBLISHERS, INC.
121 South Main Street, Chelsea, Michigan 48118

PRINTED IN THE UNITED STATES OF AMERICA

This book is dedicated to our parents
Constance and Kemon Prescott and
Mary and Morse Brossman
for their love and support.

Preface

The following scenario may be encountered by the reader:

Your company purchased an industrial site for expansion of operations. The seller and previous owners conducted unknown activities at the site that were not disclosed by the seller or investigated by your company. Soon after construction is started, buried hazardous waste drums and two underground storage tanks are found. There is evidence of extensive contamination of soils and groundwater from hazardous materials that have leaked from the drums and tanks.

Your company must now contend with investigation and cleanup of the contamination prior to continuing construction. As the current owner of the property, your company will most likely be liable for the costs of the cleanup. These costs could have been avoided had your company negotiated a comprehensive contract of sale covering future environmental liabilities with the seller prior to acquisition. Because your company did not consider potential environmental liabilities at the site or provide for protection from those liabilities in the transaction agreement, your company is now subject to investigation and cleanup costs of millions of dollars and delays in completion of construction.

This scenario illustrates one of the potentially expensive pitfalls that may result from property transfer and financing. Most of these pitfalls can be avoided, however, if appropriate steps are taken prior to completing the transaction. This book provides basic information on environmental issues, potential environmental liabilities, and how to reduce the exposure from environmental liabilities. The kinds of people for whom this book is intended include engineers, lawyers, realtors, developers, bankers, and other financiers.

Much of the information on environmental laws, regulations, and case law in this book is dynamic. Consequently, such information will be superseded as new laws are passed, regulations promulgated, and additional court cases decided. For the reader's reference the information in this book is current as of January 1990.

Michael K. Prescott
Douglas S. Brossman

Acknowledgments

The authors wish to thank the following people who provided valuable comments on drafts of this book: Jeffrey Lape, Charles McCormick, Jayne Brady, Matthew Ryan, John DiLoreto, Cynthia and Lee Cummings, and Charles Fotis.

Michael K. Prescott is a licensed professional environmental engineer with extensive experience in the environmental field. He graduated from Rensselaer Polytechnic Institute with a B.S. degree in environmental engineering in 1978. Since then, Mr. Prescott has conducted numerous environmental assessments, audits, inspections, and investigations. Mr. Prescott is a principal in the environmental consulting firm EMI Associates, Inc., based in Fairfax, Virginia, which provides environmental consultation to industry and government throughout the country.

Douglas S. Brossman, Esq., received a B.S. degree in Civil Engineering from Pennsylvania State University in 1980. He practiced as an environmental engineer until he received his Juris Doctorate degree from the Dickinson School of Law in 1985. Since then, Mr. Brossman has practiced as an environmental lawyer providing counsel to corporate, industrial, and banking clients throughout the northern Atlantic states. Mr. Brossman is associated with the law firm of Rich, Tucker & Rice in Annapolis, Maryland and currently practices law in Ephrata, Pennsylvania.

Contents

List of Tables

CHAPTER 1

Introduction

Introduction

The environmental movement and associated laws and regulations commenced in earnest less than 20 years ago. During this period, environmental laws and regulations have evolved from initial modest attempts to reduce water and air pollution to the present day control of every aspect of environmental degradation. These controls are governed by a myriad of laws and regulations implemented by federal, state and local agencies. Furthermore, beyond the maze of laws and regulations, extensive environmental case law has been developed that further defines environmental requirements and liabilities.

When the environmental movement first began, the general public did not need to be well versed in the specific aspects of environmental law — this was left to the environmental professional. Now, environmental regulation touches on every sector of the business community. In the 1990s and beyond, a basic understanding of the impacts of these environmental controls will be essential to the continued operation of any business.

Just as the scope of activities regulated by these environmental statutes has expanded, so has the scope of parties potentially liable for cleanup costs pursuant to these statutes. Congress has given the Environmental Protection Agency (EPA) broad discretion to reach into the private sector in an effort to find a "deep pocket" to finance the costs of environmental cleanup and compliance.

This book will identify the particular aspects of environmental law related to the potential environmental liability that may arise from acquiring property. This area of environmental law is relatively new, having been spawned by the hazardous waste site cleanup laws and recent court decisions that have imposed responsibility for cleanup of waste sites upon parties having nothing to do with the activities resulting in the contamination. The legislative and judicial background for environmental liability in property transfer and financing is covered in Chapter 2. Also covered in Chapter 2 are state laws which require investigation and cleanup under state supervision prior to transfer of industrial property.

The Superfund law and its amendments, policy issued by the EPA to further define and clarify the requirements of the law, and the court's interpretation of the law have essentially made the owner of a contaminated property liable for the costs of investigating and cleaning up the contamination. This liability might extend to any owner of the property, even one who was not the owner at the time waste was disposed at the property or involved in the operations resulting in the contamination. This extension of liability has become a potentially expensive discovery for subsequent owners and financiers of contaminated property. These unexpected discoveries have resulted in, at best, delays in the use of the property and, at worst, investigation and cleanup costs of millions of dollars.

The Superfund law and its amendments, as well as EPA policy, have provided a potential defense to this liability through appropriate inquiry into the past uses of the property and investigation of the site. Chapter 3 of this book provides a discussion of the scope of this defense and how best to ensure that a proper defense could be established.

The appropriate inquiry and site investigation are referred to as the environmental site assessment. Such an assessment should be done by a qualified and experienced environmental professional. The environmental site assessment consists of various technical and legal investigations to try to uncover any actual or suspected contamination of the property. The assessment also seeks to identify environmental violations of which the purchaser or lender should be aware. The activities to be conducted as part of the environmental assessment are dependent on the past and present uses of the site, as well as potential future uses. The scope of the assessment and factors to consider in contracting for the assessment are discussed in Chapter 4.

Once the environmental site assessment has been completed, a report of the findings is prepared along with recommendations for future investigations if contamination is found or suspected. Often, the site assessment presents results that only the environmental lawyer or engineer understands. If sampling and analysis of soils or wastes on-site are included in the report, the layperson will generally not know if the concentration of the pollutant found presents a potential problem, or how it may affect the transaction. Chapter 5 provides multimedia environmental standards to allow the prospective purchaser and other parties to the transaction to understand and evaluate the results of the report. Chapter 5 also includes examples of some potential environmental liabilities that are likely to be encountered.

Once the prospective purchaser or lender receives and understands the results of the site assessment, the decision becomes if and how it affects the transaction. Should further investigations be conducted? Should the deal be abandoned? Should the deal be restructured or renegotiated? Should indemnifications be sought or escrows established to fund potential future cleanup or liability? Should the purchase price be adjusted?

Chapter 6 relates the site assessment to the transaction and provides alternatives which may allow the transaction to be consummated in spite of potential environmental problems. The chapter also provides methods for protecting the interests of the buyer, seller, and lender.

It is not always clear when an environmental site assessment is needed. For the acquisition of a manufacturing plant that handles hazardous materials, an assessment is an absolute necessity. Likewise, if a corporation acquires another corporation with potentially environmentally hazardous operations (such as a chemical plant), then an assessment is needed at the corporation's active and inactive properties.

Other cases may not be as clear cut as the preceding examples. Because of recent extensions of liability as discussed below, almost any transaction will require an assessment. Such a case could involve a manufacturing plant seeking a loan to expand facilities. It would be prudent for the lender to require that an environmental site assessment be conducted.

Another example would be a developer buying land for development which was previously occupied by persons conducting unknown operations. Although the unknown operations may not have been active for many years, such a site could still be contaminated, thus presenting a potential liability. Consequently, the developer should have a site assessment performed prior to acquiring the land. If the developer does not require such a site assessment, the lender of the project probably will. Hypothetical case studies presenting various scenarios, site assessment needs, results of the assessment and potential affects on the scenario are presented in Chapter 7.

Throughout this book, we will discuss the need for prospective owners and lenders to be aware of applicable environmental laws and requirements and the need for environmental site assessments. Additionally, realtors and real estate lawyers can benefit from this information. Especially those realtors and real estate lawyers involved with commercial and industrial development. Their understanding of the need for site assessments will greatly assist when advising clients. Lawyers must also understand the potential liabilities that may be unknowingly assumed by their clients and how to structure the transaction to protect their clients' interests.

A glossary of important environmental terms, acronyms, and laws is provided after Chapter 7 to aid the reader in understanding the text of the book and as a desktop reference.

Four appendices are provided after the glossary:

1. Appendix A lists citations for key environmental statutes.
2. Appendix B presents an outline of an environmental site assessment checklist.
3. Appendix C provides a list of chemical-specific standards (referred to as ARARs) for cleanup of hazardous waste sites.
4. Appendix D contains sample contract provisions which address environmental issues.

CHAPTER 2

Legislative and Judicial Background

CHAPTER CONTENTS

Legislative and Judicial Background

2.1 INTRODUCTION

Beginning in the 1970s, an unprecedented number of environmental statutes have been passed at both the federal and state level. These extremely complex and interrelated laws not only subjected U.S. industry to an ever increasing maze of regulation on its current business operations, but also sought to impose upon the private sector the burden of remediation caused by the past acts of others.

With increasing frequency, the liabilities created by these laws are being extended to those who had nothing to do with the acts causing the environmental hazard. As a result, a prospective purchaser in today's market must not only be concerned with the economics of the transaction, but also the current environmental status of the property. Purchasers must be aware that past activities on the property have the potential of subjecting the buyer to millions of dollars of liability for past violations or remediation of contamination.

While dozens of statutes have been enacted in the last 20 years, the ones most frequently encountered in the real estate context include the Comprehensive Environmental Response, Compensation and Liability Act (CERCLA or "Superfund"), the Resource Conservation and Recovery Act (RCRA), the Clean Air Act, and the Clean Water Act (the complete citations for each of these statutes and other frequently encountered statutes are set forth in Appendix A). These statutes impose liability not only for improper discharges to land, air, surface water, groundwater, or public sewer systems, but also for the improper treatment, storage, or disposal of hazardous wastes, including those wastes which were disposed of years ago by others. This chapter provides a detailed description of each of these statutes, as well as a summary of recent judicial decisions which have further expanded their impact.

2.2 LEGISLATIVE BACKGROUND

In order to evaluate the potential environmental considerations that must be addressed in the transaction, it is necessary to be aware of the multiple statutes which may impact on-site activities or impose liability. Set forth below is a brief discussion of the major environmental laws which frequently impact real estate transactions. This summary is intended to provide a general awareness of the breadth of environmental regulation.

2.2.1 The Comprehensive Environmental Response, Compensation and Liability Act

The Comprehensive Environmental Response, Compensation and Liability Act (also known as "CERCLA" or "Superfund")[1], was passed by Congress in 1980. Congress' goal in passing CERCLA was to provide a regulatory framework to address any uncontrolled release of hazardous materials to the environment. CERCLA is intended to remediate present releases caused by past activities. CERCLA establishes the National Priorities List (NPL) whereby contaminated sites are listed and assigned a priority based upon the severity of the contamination. CERCLA may then require remediation of a listed site where a release has or is likely to occur, regardless of when the activity causing the release occurred.

After a site has been determined to be a Superfund site, the federal government is authorized to clean up the site and then seek reimbursement from responsible parties as defined in the Act. Responsible parties are also authorized to initiate the cleanup themselves and seek contribution from other responsible parties.

The continuing impact of Superfund is best evidenced by its funding history as provided by Congress. When first created in 1980, Congress generated $1.6 billion (the Superfund) to pay for government cleanups of hazardous waste sites. The Superfund was funded mostly by a special tax on the petroleum and chemical industries. The Superfund is also to be reimbursed with cleanup monies recovered from responsible parties.

In 1986, Congress passed the Superfund Amendment and Reauthorization Act (SARA), which, as implied by its name, reauthorized the original Superfund. In addition to the amendments discussed further below, SARA established an $8.5 billion fund for government-instituted cleanups. Thus, Congress has given a clear indication that Superfund liability will exist well into the future.

2.2.1.1 Scope of Liability

The impact of Superfund is apparent by a review of the breadth of potentially responsible parties ("PRPs") who may be liable for required remediation. Responsible Parties liable under Superfund include:

1. the owner or operator of the property;
2. the owner or operator of the property at the time the hazardous substances were disposed of;
3. any person who arranged for the disposal or treatment, or arranged with a transporter for transport for disposal or treatment of the hazardous substances; and
4. any person who accepts or accepted any hazardous substances for transport to disposal or treatment facilities.[2]

These Responsible Parties are liable for the following costs:

1. all costs of removal or remedial action incurred by the U.S. government or a state;
2. any other necessary costs of response incurred by any other person consistent with the National Contingency Plan;
3. damages for injury to, destruction of, or loss of natural resources, including the cost of assessing the costs of these damages; and
4. the costs of any required health assessment or health effects study.[3]

These statutory definitions demonstrate the importance of including CERCLA considerations in the real estate transaction decision. In a nutshell, these definitions impose strict, joint, and several liability for the entire cost of site cleanup on the current "owner or operator" of the site, the owner at the time of disposal, anyone who generated any of the wastes disposed of at the site, or any one who transported any wastes to the site.[4]

2.2.1.2 Imposition of Liability

As indicated above, current owners of the property will be held liable for the actions of past owners in disposing of hazardous substances on the property. The purchaser of property containing buried hazardous wastes disposed of by past owners could be liable for the entire cleanup of the property despite the fact that the new owner took no part in and had no knowledge of the disposal.[5] Because these costs will often exceed the value of the property, the prospective purchaser must take all possible steps to avoid purchasing this type of liability.

Lenders may also be held liable for the cleanup of contamination caused by the past activities of others. CERCLA includes a specific exclusion for lenders by providing that the term "owner or operator" does not include a person who, without participating in the management of the facility, holds an indicia (element) of ownership primarily to protect his security interest in the facility.[6] Lenders have been deemed "owners or operators", however, when they have participated in day-to-day activities of the site or have taken title through foreclosure.

The prospective purchaser must also be aware of potential off-site liabilities imposed by CERCLA. If as part of the transaction, the new purchaser assumes the seller's liabilities and obligations, the new purchaser may once again be buying into CERCLA liability, even if the property involved in the transaction is free of contamination. If any waste generated by the purchaser's predecessor was transported to a site that is or becomes a Superfund site, the new purchaser could be liable for the cleanup.

The application of CERCLA to a specific site, however, is subject to certain limitations. All remediation actions under CERCLA must be pursuant to the National Contingency Plan (NCP), which has been delegated to the EPA for implementation and revision.[7] The NCP requires that the EPA rank potential

Superfund sites to establish cleanup priorities. The EPA has developed the Hazard Ranking System which assigns a numerical designation to sites based upon the severity of the threat the site poses to the environment and general public.[8] If the site is assigned a hazard ranking system in excess of 28.5, the site is then placed on the National Priorities List (NPL) maintained by the EPA. Future Superfund sites are then chosen from the NPL. Thus, prospective purchasers must check the NPL not only to determine if the property to be acquired is listed, but to check for sites to which wastes from the property were sent.

2.2.1.3 Title III: Emergency Planning and Community Right-to-Know

SARA created a new provision in CERCLA known as Title III: the Emergency Planning and Community Right-to-Know Act of 1986.[9] These provisions are intended to increase the public's knowledge and access to information on the types and quantities of hazardous chemicals used in their community and the releases of those chemicals to the environment. This goal is achieved by requiring federal, state, and local government and industry to complete reports on types and quantities of hazardous materials in the workplace that may be released to the environment. This information is made available to the employees handling the materials, as well as to the community in general, thus allowing them to prepare for potential emergencies.

2.2.2 The Resource Conservation and Recovery Act

The Resource Conservation and Recovery Act (RCRA) is intended to provide a comprehensive regulatory scheme for the regulation of hazardous wastes.[10] RCRA, which was enacted by Congress in 1976 and amended in both 1980 and 1984, regulates the generation, storage, transport, and disposal of hazardous waste. The Act's objective of controlling all aspects of hazardous waste is often referred to as the "cradle to grave" regulation of hazardous waste.

The first significant aspect of RCRA is the broad definition of hazardous waste provided by the statute and the regulations promulgated thereunder.[11] The EPA has prepared lists of specific wastes it has deemed to be hazardous and subject to regulation under RCRA.[12] The EPA has also identified certain industrial processes whose waste streams are also designated as hazardous.[13] Finally, if the waste demonstrates any one of four hazardous characteristics defined by the EPA (corrosivity, ignitability, reactivity, or toxicity), the waste is also deemed hazardous.[14]

RCRA is implemented pursuant to strict operating and recordkeeping requirements. Any industry which generates hazardous waste must obtain a hazardous waste identification number from the EPA.[15] The generator must keep copious records as to the volumes, types, and disposition of hazardous waste generated. In addition, RCRA specifies requirements for managing the wastes, training personnel, and developing capabilities for responding to emergencies. If the hazardous waste is to be stored at the facility in excess of 90 days, the company must obtain a facility permit authorizing the storage of hazardous waste.[16]

Any hazardous waste transported off-site must be shipped according to information on the accompanying manifest.[17] This manifest lists the type and quantity of the waste, the generator, the transporter, and the ultimate site of treatment or disposal (TSD facility). The manifest must be signed by all parties who handle the waste between generation and ultimate treatment or disposal (thus the "cradle to grave" designation). Copies of the manifest must be maintained by the generator, transporter, and TSD facility. Copies of the manifests, as well as annual generator reports, must also be submitted to the EPA and the appropriate state authority.[18]

RCRA also establishes stiff penalties for failure to comply with operating or recordkeeping requirements. Companies which violate RCRA may be liable for civil penalties of up to $25,000 per day.[19] Violators may also be subject to criminal sanctions.[20] Thus, prospective purchasers must determine if current operations on the property are subject to the requirements of RCRA, and if any past violations by past operators remain outstanding.

RCRA also includes provisions allowing the EPA to issue an administrative order requiring site remediation when the EPA determines that an imminent hazard exists.[21] These provisions have been used in recent years in parallel with CERCLA to require cleanup of a site contaminated by actions of past owners.[22] By proceeding pursuant to RCRA instead of CERCLA, the EPA can take action against a site which has not been listed on the NPL or assigned a hazard ranking, thereby providing more flexibility to the EPA in determining which sites require remediation. This bypassing of the NPL requirement allows the EPA to require remediation at many more sites, including many smaller sites which, because of their size, would not be high priority sites if listed on the NPL. The other significant difference is that states which have been delegated authority by the EPA to implement the provisions of RCRA are also given broad remediation authority by RCRA's imminent hazard provisions. Thus, even though a site is not listed on the NPL, the owner of the property may still be exposed to significant cleanup costs under RCRA.

The 1984 amendments to RCRA added an additional element that has had a significant impact on real estate transactions. These amendments created a new Subtitle I which established a complete regulatory scheme for the control of underground storage tanks.[23] Regulations promulgated pursuant to this Subtitle have established stringent construction standards for new underground storage tanks.[24] Further, these regulations created extensive reporting requirements for existing tanks, as well as stringent procedures to be followed for removing or discontinuing use of tanks. If an underground storage tank has been found to be leaking, the owner or operator of the facility must notify the appropriate regulatory authority of the release.[25] Failure to comply with the underground storage tank regulations is a violation of RCRA subjecting the owner or operator to substantial civil and/or criminal penalties.

2.2.3 The Clean Water Act

The Federal Water Pollution Control Act, passed in 1972 and subsequently amended in 1977, 1982, and 1987, is now commonly known as the Clean Water Act (CWA).[26] The CWA establishes a statutory framework regulating the discharge of pollutants into "waters of the United States." As applied to industry, the CWA regulates the discharge of all process wastewaters to open waters (known as direct discharges) or public sewer systems (known as indirect discharges). The CWA prohibits the discharge of any pollutant to waters of the United States without an appropriate discharge permit.[27] To implement this permit requirement, the EPA has developed the National Pollutant Discharge Elimination System (NPDES) which provides for the issuance of discharge permits by EPA or appropriate state agencies.[28]

Under the CWA, EPA developed regulations that established technology-based effluent discharge standards. These standards were developed by analyzing specific industrial categories and processes to determine the "Best Practical," "Best Conventional," and "Best Available" treatment technologies for these processes.[29] EPA then applied these treatment technologies to the process wastewaters to determine the appropriate discharge standards for each industrial process.[30]

A plant which generates process wastewaters must obtain an NPDES permit to discharge those wastewaters. If the plant is unable to meet the discharge standards established by the EPA or state agency, it must either discontinue the discharge or improve its treatment works to meet the effluent standards. Where EPA has not established discharge standards for a specific type of industrial process, the EPA or state agency will apply a "best professional judgment" standard based on available data on the known pollutants in the discharge.[31]

Even if a plant is able to meet the required effluent discharge limitations, the plant may be subject to more stringent limitations if it is determined that the discharge may violate state water quality standards or federal water quality criteria for the receiving waters.[32]

In addition to meeting permit discharge criteria, the permittee is also subject to certain monitoring and reporting requirements. The permittee is required to monitor its discharge to ensure that it complies with the discharge standards established in the permit.[33] The permittee must also prepare Discharge Monitoring Reports (DMRs), usually submitted to the regulatory agencies on a quarterly basis. These DMRs set forth the results of the permittee's monitoring program. Any known violations of permit conditions would be indicated on the DMRs. Further, it should also be noted that any known discharge violations must also be reported to the regulatory agency within 24 hours of becoming aware of the violation.

The CWA also regulates discharges to public sewerage systems (referred to as "publicly owned treatment works" or POTWs) through regulations known as "Pretreatment Regulations."[34] These regulations control the discharges from industrial facilities to POTWs to prevent any discharge that may interfere with operations at the treatment plant and or pose a hazard to the receiving waters. EPA has also developed technology-based standards for certain industrial categories and processes equivalent to the standards developed for direct discharges described above. Even if a facility's discharge complies with the local sewer authority's regulations, failure to comply with federal pretreatment regulations for the specific discharge is still a violation of federal law.

Discharging pollutants to waters of the United States in violation of the CWA could subject the discharger to significant civil and/or criminal penalties. These penalties are as high as $25,000 per day and also may include imprisonment.[35] Further, failure to comply with the reporting requirements or failure to submit the DMRs is also a violation of the CWA. Finally, even if past violations have been corrected, the permittee may still be liable for significant penalties that accrued during the period of noncompliance.

2.2.4 The Clean Air Act

The Clean Air Act (CAA) establishes the statutory framework whereby the EPA may regulate industrial discharges of pollutants to air.[36] The CAA was first passed by Congress in 1970 and amended in 1977. The CAA seeks to regulate discharges to the air by establishing three sets of standards:

1. National Ambient Air Quality Standards;[37]
2. Standards of Performance for New Stationary Sources;[38]
3. National Emissions Standards for Hazardous Air Pollutants (NESHAPs).[39]

These emission requirements are then implemented on a regional basis. The extent of emission regulation is dependent on the area in which the activity is located and the ambient air quality within that area.

2.2.5 The Toxic Substances Control Act

The Toxic Substances Control Act (TSCA) was passed in 1976 to regulate certain chemical substances that pose "unreasonable risk of injury to health or the environment."[40] The two substances regulated under TSCA are asbestos and polychlorinated biphenyls (PCBs). Generally, TSCA seeks to remove PCBs from the workplace by phasing in prohibitions as to the manufacture, import, or distribution of PCBs. Title III of TSCA establishes the Asbestos Hazard Emergency Response Act of 1986 (AHERA), which provides a stringent regulatory framework for inspection and abatement of asbestos-containing materials in schools. In the future, these activities may be expanded to include commercial buildings as well.

2.3 JUDICIAL INTERPRETATIONS

Set forth above is a summary of environmental legislation that has the potential for imposing significant liability on a purchaser of real property. This section discusses how recent judicial interpretations have imposed liability.

2.3.1 Subsequent Purchaser Liability

As applied to real estate transactions, the prospective purchaser is most concerned about being deemed an "owner or operator" of a hazardous waste site. If the new purchaser is deemed to be an owner or operator, the overwhelming majority of cases have held that joint and several liability may be imposed, thereby subjecting the new owner to the entire cost of the cleanup.[41] This strict, joint, and several liability covers costs incurred prior to the passage of CERCLA.[42]

In *New York v. Shore Realty*,[43] the defendant purchased the subject property with the intent to develop the property. The property had been significantly contaminated by past activities. The new purchaser of the property, Shore Realty Corp., was found liable for the cleanup costs, even though it did not own the property at the time of the contamination, and had nothing to do with the activities resulting in the contamination. This conclusion has been continually confirmed in the courts.[44]

2.3.2 Lease Liability

The lessor of property has also been held to be an owner of the property and liable for the cleanup of contamination caused solely by the lessee. In *United States v. Argent*,[45] the owner leased the property to a company that treated and stored hazardous materials. The court held that because the lessor had knowledge of the lessee's activities, the lessor could be held liable under CERCLA for the remediation of contamination caused by the lessee, even though there was no involvement by the lessor in the business of the waste company. In a similar case, however, the court in *United States v. South Carolina Recycling, Inc.*[46] reached a different conclusion. There the court found that because the lessee had total control of the property, the lessee stood in the shoes of the owner.

The lessor of property may also be liable for cleanup of contamination caused solely by the activities of the lessee. In *United States v. Monsanto Co.*,[47] the subject site was contaminated solely by the acts of the lessee, without the knowledge of the lessor. Because CERCLA imposes liability on the "owner" of the facility, the court held that the absentee lessor was jointly and severally liable for the costs of the cleanup. A similar decision was also reached in *United States v. Northernaire Plating Co.*[48]

2.3.3 Corporate Liability

Successor corporations have also been held liable for the acts of a predecessor corporation. In *State Dept. of Environ. Protect. v. Ventron*,[49] a parent corporation was held liable for the acts of its wholly owned subsidiary. This line of cases would indicate that where one company purchases all the stock of another corporation, or where one corporation merges into another corporation, the successor will be liable for the cleanup of any contamination caused by the activities of the predecessor corporation. Further, if the transaction involved only a transfer of assets, cleanup liability may be imposed if the transfer also included an assumption of liabilities. In the recent case of *Anspec Co. v. Johnson Controls, Inc.*,[50] however, the U.S. District Court for the Eastern District of Michigan has held that successor corporate liability does not apply to site cleanups pursuant to CERCLA.

Parent corporations have also been held liable for contamination caused solely by their wholly owned subsidiaries. In *United States v. Kayser-Roth Corp.*,[51] the court held that the parent corporation exercised pervasive control over the subsidiary's operations, including the power to control the release of contamination and authority to prevent and abate environmental damage. In holding the parent liable, the court reasoned that a uniform federal rule should be applied in CERCLA cases involving the piercing of the corporate veil. A contrary decision was reached in *Joslyn Manufacturing Co. v. T. L. James & Co.*,[52] however, where the court held a parent not liable for the violations of its subsidiary. In *Joslyn,* the daily operations of the parent and subsidiary were kept separate. As a result, the court refused to pierce the corporate veil, holding that the legislative history of CERCLA does not demonstrate any intent on the part of Congress to alter traditional corporate law doctrines.

The courts have also held that individual liability may be imposed on the owners of a corporation by piercing the corporate veil. In *United States v. Mottolo*,[53] the defendant incorporated his business in an effort to avoid individual liability. The court held that although the corporate entity is generally recognized, it may not be used to override federal legislative policies and will be disregarded in the interests of public convenience, fairness, and equity. Because CERCLA's goal is to impose liability on those causing the contamination, the court concluded that CERCLA places no importance on the corporate form. Thus, it does not provide absolute protection to its shareholders.

Officers, directors, and major shareholders of corporations involved in day-to-day corporate activities have also been held personally liable for remediation costs. In *United States v. NEPACCO*,[54] the court found that a corporate officer and owner of the corporation may be individually liable under CERCLA if the officer was personally involved in the actions giving rise to the liability. A major shareholder of a corporation was also held individually responsible because the shareholder was personally involved in the manufacturing of chemicals and the actual improper placement of wastes. Finally, in *United States v. Conservation Chemical Co.*,[55] the court held that a corporate officer of the parent corporation who formed a subsidiary corporation, served as its chief executive officer and majority stockholder, and was personally involved in many of the activities leading to contamination was personally liable under CERCLA.

2.3.4 Lender Liability

Lenders are also not free from liability under CERCLA. The first case in which a lender was found liable was *United States v. Mirabile*.[56] There, the EPA sought reimbursement of remediation costs incurred in 1983 from Mirabile, the then current owner of the site. Mirabile had acquired the site in 1981 from American Bank and Trust, who foreclosed on the property pursuant to the terms of a 1976 mortgage it held on the property. Mirabile impleaded American Bank and Trust, as well as Girard Bank (predecessor to Mellon Bank), who also loaned money to the former operation in 1981. Both banks sought to be dismissed. The court, in dismissing the claims against American Bank and Trust, held that American Bank and Trust's actions were aimed solely at protecting its collateral. Thus, American Bank and Trust was exempted from liability under CERCLA. The court did not dismiss Girard, however, finding that Girard was involved in the day-to-day operations of the site. Girard had installed an officer of the bank on the site as a "work out" officer. He made frequent visits to the site and passed on all operational decisions. As a result, Girard was found to be an operator of the site, and thereby liable under CERCLA.

The second case finding lender liability was *United States v. Maryland Bank and Trust*,[57] which went well beyond the holding in Mirabile. In that case, Maryland Bank and Trust Co. took title to the subject property at a foreclosure sale it conducted in 1981. In 1983, the EPA cleaned up the site under CERCLA and sought reimbursement from the bank. The court held that Maryland Bank and Trust's actions in taking title at foreclosure merged its security interest into the real title to the property. As a result, the court reasoned that the bank was no longer operating solely to protect its security interest, but instead was an owner/operator of the site and therefore subject to liability under CERCLA.

Other actions, short of foreclosure on the property, might also subject the lender to liability under CERCLA. In *United States v. Fleet Factors Corp.*,[58] the defendant held a security interest in both the facility and certain equipment and inventory of the owner. Although the lender did not foreclose on the facility, it did foreclose on the equipment and inventory. While the court held that the lender's activities prior to the foreclosure did not make the lender an "owner or operator" liable under CERCLA, the lender may be liable for response costs incurred in connection with the equipment sale. Because the lender's contractor may have moved barrels containing hazardous substances before conducting the equipment sale which may have contributed friable asbestos, the lender may be liable for response costs of cleanup.

These cases demonstrate the extent of potential liability which may attach under CERCLA. Owners, operators, lenders, lessees, or lessors may be held liable for actual or potential contamination caused solely by the acts of others. Thus, this potential liability should be investigated prior to any acquisition.

2.4 STATE LAWS

Many states have passed their own Superfund statutes that act, to varying degrees, in parallel with the federal Superfund law. One significant difference between CERCLA and many state superfund programs is the creation of what is commonly referred to as a "superlien." These provisions allow the state to impose a lien against a company to cover the costs of site cleanup. In some states, this lien covers not only the subject site, but also other property owned by the company. Further, whereas liens filed under CERCLA are subject to the rights of prior creditors, some state statutes create superliens that are superior to prior creditors' liens.

In an effort to provide uniformity to the environmental issues considered in real estate transactions, some states have passed laws defining the scope of investigation that must be performed prior to the transfer of industrial property. The first state to enact such a law was New Jersey, which in 1983 passed the Environmental Cleanup and Responsibility Act (ECRA).[59]

ECRA applies to the transfer of any property in New Jersey which has been involved in the handling of any hazardous substances. Prior to the transfer, the transferor must submit a negative declaration to the New Jersey Department of Environmental Protection (DEP) certifying that there has been no discharge of hazardous substances or wastes on or from the industrial establishment, or that any discharge on or from the industrial establishment has been remediated. The transfer cannot be completed until the negative declaration is approved from the DEP.

If the site is determined to be contaminated, the transferor must develop a remediation plan designed to clean up the site. This cleanup must either be completed prior to the transfer or be sufficiently bonded to guarantee completion of the remediation plan. In this latter situation, the purchaser must assume responsibility to continue the cleanup if the initial bond proves insufficient to cover cleanup costs.

An increasing number of states are adopting legislation requiring environmental property evaluations prior to transfer. A recent count indicated that nine states have passed legislation, with an additional 21 states considering the issue.

2.5 COMMON LAW CLAIMS

In addition to the liabilities imposed by federal laws and their state counterparts, state common law may also impose liability for damage to property and personal injury. The predominate common law theories used to impose liability include negligence, trespass, and nuisance. Negligence imposes liability based upon a "reasonable standard," with what is "reasonable" being governed by the circumstances as they exist at the time. Trespass includes a physical invasion of the property of another which interferes with the latter's use of his property. Nuisance is defined as unreasonable interference with another's use and enjoyment of his property.

In addition to these three common law theories, recent common law has spawned a new theory assigning strict liability to a party under certain circumstances. This theory has been used to designate the handling of hazardous materials as being "ultrahazardous" and consequently subject the party handling the hazardous materials to a strict liability standard.

The final area of concern is "Toxic Torts." Where a party's handling of hazardous materials causes human exposure resulting in personal injury, those persons injured may have a claim against the party causing the exposure. Toxic tort claims generally involve severe long-term injury to a large group of people. As a result, toxic tort liability may be significant. Further, because the type of injuries encountered do not immediately manifest themselves, this potential liability may not surface for many years.

2.6 CONCLUSION

This chapter outlines recent environmental legislation that may impose significant environmental liability on the purchaser of real estate. This liability may be imposed even if the purchaser had no involvement in the activities causing the contamination, and regardless of whether or not the purchaser had actual knowledge of the contamination. This liability may also be imposed on lessors when the contamination results from the actions of the lessee, or upon lenders when the contamination results from the actions of the borrower.

While this liability may be significant, there are methods which the purchaser can employ to protect himself. These defenses are explained in the following chapter.

REFERENCES

1. United States Code, Vol. 42, Sec. 9601 *et seq.*
2. United States Code, Vol. 42, Sec. 9606.
3. *Id.*

4. *United States v. Monsanto Co.*, 858 F.2d 160 (4th Cir. 1988); *United States v. Northernaire*, 670 F. Supp. 472 (W.D.Mich. 1987).
5. *Tanglewood East Homeowners' Assn. v. Charles Thomas, Inc.*, 849 F.2d 1568 (5th Cir. 1988); *New York v. Shore Realty Corp.*, 759 F.2d 1032 (2d Cir. 1985); *United States v. Hooker Chemical and Plastics Corp.*, 680 F. Supp. 546 (W.D.N.Y. 1988).
6. United States Code, Vol. 42, Sec. 9601(20).
7. United States Code, Vol. 42, Sec. 9605.
8. U.S. Code of Federal Regulations, Vol 40, Part 300, Appendix A (1988).
9. United States Code, Vol. 42, Sec. 11001 *et seq.*
10. United States Code, Vol. 42, Sec. 6901 *et seq.*
11. United States Code, Vol. 42, Sec. 6903(5); U.S. Code of Federal Regulations, Vol. 40, Part 261 (1988).
12. U.S. Code of Federal Regulations, Vol. 40, Part 261 (1988).
13. *Id.*
14. *Id.*
15. U.S. Code of Federal Regulations, Vol. 40, Part 262 (1988).
16. *Id.*
17. *Id.*
18. *Id.*
19. United States Code, Vol. 42. Sec. 6928.
20. *Id.*
21. United States Code, Vol. 42, Sec. 6973.
22. *Smith Land & Improvement Corp. v. Celotex Corp.*, 851 F.2d 86 (3rd Cir. 1988).
23. United States Code, Vol. 42, Sec. 6991 *et seq.*
24. U.S. Code of Federal Regulations, Vol. 40, Part 280 (1988).
25. *Id.*
26. United States Code, Vol. 33, Sec. 1251 *et seq.*
27. United States Code, Vol. 33, Sec. 1342.
28. *Id.*
29. U.S. Code of Federal Regulations, Vol. 40, Part 400 *et seq.* (1988).
30. *Id.*
31. U.S. Code of Federal Regulations, Vol. 40, Part 122 *et seq.* (1988).
32. U.S. Code of Federal Regulations, Vol. 40, Part 122 (1988).
33. U.S. Code of Federal Regulations, Vol. 40, Part 122 *et seq.* (1988).
34. U.S. Code of Federal Regulations, Vol. 40, Part 403 (1988).
35. United States Code, Vol. 33, Sec. 1319.
36. United States Code, Vol. 40, Sec. 7401 *et seq.*
37. United States Code, Vol. 40, Sec. 7409.
38. United States Code, Vol. 40, Sec. 7411.
39. United States Code, Vol. 40, Sec. 7412.
40. United States Code, Vol. 15, Sec. 2601 *et seq.*
41. *United States v. Chem-Dyne Corp.*, 572 F.Supp. 802 (D.Ohio 1983); *United States v. Ottati & Goss, Inc.*, 630 F.Supp. 1361 (D.N.H. 1986).

42. *United States v. Hooker Chemicals and Plastics Corp.*, 680 F.Supp. 546 (W.D.N.Y. 1988).
43. *New York v. Shore Realty,* 759 F.2d 1032 (2d Cir. 1985).
44. *Tanglewood East Homeowners' Assn. v. Charles Thomas, Inc.*, 849 F.2d 1568 (5th Cir. 1988); *PVO International, Inc. v. Drew Chemical Corp.*, 19 E.L.R. 20077 (D.N.J. 1988).
45. *United States v. Argent Corp.*, 14 E.L.R. 20616 (D.N.M. 1984).
46. *United States v. South Carolina Recycling, Inc.*, 14 E.L.R. 20895 (D.S.C. 1984).
47. *United States v. Monsanto Co.*, 858 F.2d 160 (4th Cir. 1988)
48. *United States v. Northernaire Plating Co.*, 670 F.Supp. 742 (W.D.Mich. 1987).
49. *State Dept. of Environ. Protect. v. Ventron*, 468 A.2d 150 (N.J. 1983).
50. *Anspec Co. v. Johnson Controls, Inc.*, No. 89-CV-71165-DT (E.D. Mich., Sept. 25, 1989).
51. *United States v. Kayser-Roth Corp.*, 724 F.Supp. 15 (D.R.I. 1989).
52. *Joslyn Manufacturing Co. v. T. L. James & Co.*, No. 88-4901 (5th Cir. Jan. 29, 1990).
53. *United States v. Mottolo*, 14 E.L.R. 20497 (D.N.H. 1984).
54. *United States v. Northeastern Pharmaceutical Co.*, 810 F.2d 726 (8th Cir. 1986).
55. *United States v. Conservation Chemical*, 628 F.Supp 391 (W.D.Mo. 1986).
56. *United States v. Mirabile*, 15 E.L.R. 20992 (E.D.Pa. 1985).
57. *United States v. Maryland Bank & Trust*, 632 F.Supp. 573 (D.Md. 1986).
58. *United States v. Fleet Factors Corp.*, 19 E.L.R. 20529 (S.D.Ga. 1988).
59. N.J. Stat. Ann. Sec. 13:1K-6 *et seq.* (1983).

CHAPTER 3

Defenses and Protection from Liability

CHAPTER CONTENTS

Defenses and Protection from Liability

3.1 INTRODUCTION

The previous chapter discussed the environmental statutes used by federal and state regulatory agencies to impose environmental liability upon purchasers of real estate. Liability may extend to subsequent owners regardless of their involvement in the activities that caused the contamination. This chapter will discuss the methods available to prospective purchasers, lenders, lessors, or lessees to avoid or limit this potential liability to the extent possible.

3.2 STATUTORY DEFENSES TO CERCLA LIABILITY

As discussed in Chapter 2, CERCLA imposes liability on the owner or operator of a facility from which there is a "release or threatened release" of a hazardous substance.[1] The courts have consistently held that liability under CERCLA is strict, joint, and several.[2,3] Thus, to establish a case of liability, the government does not need to prove that the owner or operator contributed to the release or threat of release in any manner.

CERCLA provides four affirmative defenses, however, where liability may be avoided. Section 107(b) of the Act provides that a defendant otherwise liable under the provisions of CERCLA can escape liability if it can be established "by a preponderance of the evidence" that the release or threat of release of a hazardous substance and the damages resulting therefrom were caused solely by:

1. an act of God;
2. an act of war;
3. an act or omission of a third party; or
4. any combination of the foregoing paragraphs.[4]

The courts have consistently held that these defenses are exclusive and are to be narrowly construed.[5] Discussed below is the practical availability of the third party defense.

3.2.1 Third Party Defense

Of the statutory defenses listed above, the "third party defense" is the defense most likely to be used by a defendant who had no involvement in the activity causing the contamination. To qualify for this defense, the defendant must establish by a preponderance of the evidence that:

1. the release or threat of release was caused solely by an act or omission of a third party other than an employee or agent of the defendant, or one whose act or omission occurs in connection with a contractual relationship, existing directly or indirectly, with the defendant;
2. he exercised due care with respect to the hazardous substance concerned, taking into consideration the characteristics of such hazardous substance, in light of all relevant facts and circumstances; and
3. he took precautions against foreseeable acts or omissions of any such third party and the consequences that could foreseeably result from such acts or omissions.[6]

While this defense appears at first to be relatively broad, the defense is, in practice, severely limited by the requirement that the "third party" be someone other than one whose act or omission occurs in connection with a contractual relationship. Except as discussed below, EPA has interpreted "contractual relationship" to include a real estate deed. As a result, subsequent owners in the chain of title with the owner causing the contamination are unable to use the third party defense to avoid liability.

Owners who lease the property to third parties who contaminate the site are also unable to claim the third party defense.[7] In this situation, the lease constitutes a sufficient contractual relationship between the innocent owner and the polluting party to preclude the defense.

The third party defense was claimed by the defendant in *New York v. Shore Realty Corp.*[8] There, Shore Realty Corp., recent purchasers of the property, sought to avoid liability for the remediation of contamination caused by former tenants of the property. In denying the defendant's motion, the court held that the defendant knew of the tenants' activities before buying the property, and thus could have readily foreseen that the tenants would continue to dump hazardous materials on the property. Therefore, Shore Realty Corp. was found liable even though it did not contribute to the release.

3.2.2 Innocent Purchaser Defense (The "Due Diligence" Test)

Prior to the 1986 amendments to CERCLA (commonly referred to as SARA), the EPA took the position that a real estate deed constituted a contractual relationship, and therefore eliminated the availability of the third party defense for a landowner in the chain of title with a party who caused or contributed to the subject contamination.[9] This position has been upheld by the courts.[10]

Congress recognized that this strict liability would cause inequitable results by imposing liability on new landowners who had acquired the property for full market value and not contributed to the hazardous waste disposal activities. As a result, Congress expanded the scope of the statutory third party defense in SARA by specifically defining the term "contractual relationship" to include:[11]

> [L]and contracts, deeds or other instruments transferring title or possession, unless the real property on which the facility concerned is located was acquired by the defendant after the disposal or placement of hazardous substances on, in, or at the facility, and one or more of the [following] circumstances are also established by the defendant by a preponderance of the evidence:
>
> (i)   At the time the defendant acquired the facility the defendant did not know and had no reason to know that any hazardous substance which is the subject of the release or threatened release was disposed of on, in, or at the facility.
> (ii) The defendant is a government entity which acquired the facility by escheat, or through any other involuntary transfer or acquisition, or through the exercise of eminent domain authority by purchase or condemnation.
> (iii) The defendant acquired the facility by inheritance or bequest.

While Congress confirmed the EPA's position that a deed may constitute a contractual relationship under CERCLA, Congress also provided a framework whereby an innocent purchaser could avoid liability. Essentially, SARA requires that the prospective purchaser exercise "due diligence" in investigating a property for the presence of hazardous substances prior to the purchase of the property.

SARA also provides guidance as to the appropriate scope of inquiry to be made prior to the acquisition of the property by providing that:[12]

> To establish that the defendant had no reason to know of [the release or threatened release of hazardous substances existing on the property], the defendant must have undertaken, at the time of acquisition, all appropriate inquiry into the previous ownership and uses of the property consistent with good commercial or customary practice in an effort to minimize liability. For purposes of the preceding sentence the court shall take into account any specialized knowledge or experience on the part of the defendant, the relationship of the purchase price to the value of the property if uncontaminated, commonly known or reasonably ascertainable information about the property, the obviousness of the presence of contamination at the property, and the ability to detect such contamination by appropriate inspection.

Guidance provided by the EPA regarding the interpretation of these regulations indicates that a determination as to what constitutes "all appropriate inquiry" under all the circumstances is to be made on a case-by-case basis.[13] Generally, the EPA has indicated that it would require a more comprehensive inquiry for those involved in commercial transactions than for those involved in residential transactions for personal use.

The scope of the "appropriate inquiry" is determined by the generally accepted business practices in existence at the time of the transfer. The

Congressional Conference Committee Report provides that a reasonable inquiry must have been made "in light of best business and land transfer principles."[14] This Report also provides that the duty to inquire will be judged at the time of acquisition, and that as public awareness of environmental hazard increases, the burden of inquiry will also increase.[15] This position has been affirmed by the U.S. District Court for the Middle District of Pennsylvania.[16]

EPA guidance specifies that information to be provided to establish the innocent purchaser defense includes the following:[17]

1. evidence relevant to the actual or constructive knowledge of the landowner at the time of acquisition;
2. affirmative steps taken by the landowner to determine previous ownership and uses of the property;
3. condition of the property at the time of transfer;
4. representations made at the time of transfer;
5. purchase price of the property;
6. fair market value of comparable property at the time of transfer; and
7. any specialized knowledge of the landowner.

The landowner must also establish that upon learning of the actual or threatened release of contamination, he exercised due care regarding the release and did not contribute to the release.

If the purchaser acquires the property with actual or constructive knowledge of the contamination, the innocent purchaser defense will not be available. Constructive knowledge of the contamination will be imposed on the purchaser if a reasonable investigation of the property would have revealed the contamination or a reduced purchase price was paid for the property. As a further caveat, it would also appear that this section would provide a defense only to on-site liability. Thus, if one's corporate predecessors were found liable as a generator for off-site liability, it would appear that this defense would not be available.

Lenders must also be aware of these "due diligence" provisions. A lender who only holds an "indicia of ownership primarily to protect his security interest" and does not participate in the management of the facility is excepted from the definition of "owner or operator" and is therefore exempted from liability under CERCLA.[18] Where the lender's personnel have taken part in the day-to-day operations of the facility, or where the lender has acquired title through foreclosure, the lender may be found to be an owner or operator of the facility liable under CERCLA.[19] As a result, in order to qualify for the "due diligence" defense, the lender must take steps to satisfy the "appropriate inquiry" standard at both the time of initial acquisition and at the time of foreclosure.

SARA also provides that a landowner who acquires the property by inheritance or bequest without knowledge is not in a "contractual relationship" with prior owners. [20] The Congressional Conference Report that accompanied

SARA's passage and lays out a detailed account of congressional intent, however, indicates that the appropriate inquiry requirement is still applicable. This Report provides that those who acquire property through inheritance or bequest may rely on this defense if they engage in a reasonable inquiry, but they need not be held to the same standard as those who acquire property as part of a commercial or private transaction.[21]

The courts are beginning to provide guidance as to the appropriate scope of inquiry required to qualify for the innocent purchaser defense. The purchaser's failure to inspect the property prior to acquisition has been held to not preclude the application of the defense if common practice at the time of transfer would not normally have included a site inspection.[22] Similarly, the purchaser's assumption of seller's obligations under a state consent order does not, by itself, impose constructive knowledge of the contamination on the purchaser to preclude the defense.[23] In a more recent case, however, a purchaser's failure to inspect the property after gaining knowledge of previous industrial uses of the property was held to prevent the purchaser from asserting the innocent purchaser defense.[24]

The importance of the environmental site assessment was also discussed in *BCW Associates, Ltd. v. Occidental Chemical Corp.*[25] There, the purchaser had two separate site assessments conducted prior to acquisition. Both assessments concluded that the property was free of contamination. After acquisition, however, the owner discovered lead contamination on the property. In rejecting the purchaser's assertion of the innocent purchaser defense, the court held that a site assessment alone does not provide dispositive evidence that the owner conducted all appropriate inquiry prior to acquisition. Thus, the purchaser cannot hide behind a site assessment if he has reason to suspect its findings or require additional investigations.

Congress is also taking steps to clarify the scope of appropriate inquiry required to qualify for the defense. Legislation is currently pending that would establish a rebuttable presumption that the purchaser made appropriate inquiry if he can establish that a Phase I assessment was conducted prior to acquisition. The legislation also provides detailed a description of what must be included in the assessment.

3.2.3 *De Minimis* Settlement Alternatives

Through SARA, Congress has directed the EPA to make reasonable efforts to settle CERCLA claims against property owners who had nothing to do with the activities resulting in the contamination. CERCLA, as amended by SARA, provides that "whenever practicable and in the public interest," the government "shall as promptly as possible reach a final settlement" if the settlement "involves only a minor portion of the response costs at the facility concerned."[26]

To qualify for a *de minimis* settlement, the EPA must determine that one of the following is true:

1. the parties' contribution of waste to the site was small when compared to other wastes at the site; or
2. the party is the owner of the property where the facility is located and that the party did not permit or contribute to the activities causing the contamination.

CERCLA provides that these settlement provisions are not available to the land owner if the party purchased the property "with actual or constructive knowledge that the property was used for the generation, transportation, storage, treatment, or disposal of any hazardous substance."

Guidance provided by the EPA indicates that the requirements that must be satisfied to qualify for a *de minimis* settlement are substantially the same as the elements that must be proved at trial in order for a landowner to establish the innocent purchaser defense described above.[27] The guidance is not clear, however, whether it is knowledge of past handling of hazardous materials on the property or knowledge of an actual or potential release that would prevent a *de minimis* settlement. The literal reading of the statute would indicate that if an investigation of the property revealed that past uses of the property involved the handling of hazardous substances, a *de minimis* settlement would not be available, even if that investigation indicated that no actual or potential release exists.

The advantage of the *de minimis* settlement over the innocent purchaser defense is that it can be used administratively, prior to litigation. The innocent purchaser defense is an affirmative defense the defendant must establish at trial. The *de minimis* settlement, however, is a mechanism the EPA may use to resolve the liability of landowners prior to or in the early stages of litigation.

EPA guidance provides that the Agency will make an effort in the early stages of a case to determine whether or not a landowner satisfies the elements necessary to establish a third party defense. Such a determination may be made from information available to and under development by the Agency to identify all potentially responsible parties for the site. The EPA acknowledges that it serves no purpose to require a landowner who satisfies the elements of the third party defense to incur unnecessary litigation costs. Thus, the Agency will entertain an offer for a *de minimis* settlement prior to litigation if it determines that the landowner has a persuasive case that each of the elements has been met.

Similarly, lenders may also be eligible for the *de minimis* settlement provisions. As discussed above, a lender may become an owner of a facility by foreclosing and taking title to the property. The lender could also be deemed an operator if it conducts management activities at the site. Either of these designations could subject the lender to potential liability. EPA guidance provides, however, that the lender may be eligible for a *de minimis* settlement if, among the other criteria discussed above, it conducted "all appropriate inquiry" prior to foreclosure.

The *de minimis* settlement is also important in the context of a real estate lease. The EPA has taken the position that "owner" for the purposes of CERCLA liability includes a "lessee." EPA guidance provides that a lessee of a facility who is potentially liable as an owner may be eligible for a *de minimis* settlement provided the lessee conducted "all appropriate inquiry" prior to taking possession of the property pursuant to the lease.

The EPA has made it clear that the terms of a *de minimis* settlement will depend on the likelihood that the landowner will be able to successfully establish the innocent purchaser defense at trial.[28] If the landowner has a persuasive argument, the terms of the settlement might only require that the landowner provide access to the property, as well as assurances that the landowner will exercise due care with respect to the release or threat of release. Depending on the strength of the landowner's case, the EPA might seek a cash contribution as part of the settlement agreement. The EPA will also require that the landowner file a notice in the local land records office stating that hazardous substances were disposed of on the site and that the EPA makes no representations as to the appropriate use of the property.

The settlement agreement will also contain "reopener" language that would allow the EPA to assert additional claims against the landowner.[29] The settlement will require the landowner to certify as to the accuracy of the information provided to the EPA to establish the basis for the *de minimis* settlement.

The settlement would also allow the EPA to assert additional claims or file a federal lien against the property if information not known at the time of settlement is discovered indicating that the landowner no longer would qualify for the *de minimis* settlement. The settlement will also preserve the EPA's rights to seek further relief for:

1. additional wastes deposited on the site after settlement;
2. failure of landowner to exercise due care;
3. aggravation of release by actions of landowner; or
4. landowner's failure to cooperate with the EPA.

Thus, the EPA will not provide a blanket release of all liability for the property.

3.2.4 Covenants Not to Sue

In guidance issued by the EPA, it was reported that many prospective purchasers have contacted the Agency prior to acquisition seeking a covenant not to sue whereby the EPA would covenant not to seek response costs from the new owner. Although the EPA has taken the position that it will not generally become involved in private transactions, the EPA will consider a covenant not to sue a prospective purchaser if an enforcement action is anticipated and payment from other parties is unlikely.[30] The EPA will not consider such a covenant unless a release or threatened release of pollutants is already known to exist on the property.

The EPA has established minimum criteria significantly limiting the availability of the covenant. Before the Agency will consider providing a covenant, it must determine that:

1. an enforcement action is already anticipated at the facility;
2. a substantial benefit, not otherwise available, will be received by the Agency for the cleanup;
3. the continuation of operations at the facility will not aggravate or contribute to the existing contamination;
4. the continued operation or new development of the property does not adversely impact the health of those persons likely to be present on the site; and
5. the prospective purchaser is financially viable.

Essentially, the EPA will not agree to provide a covenant not to sue unless the Agency is already considering enforcement against the property and it is unlikely that any remediation costs will be recovered from the present owner or other responsible parties. When these determinations are made, the EPA will provide a prospective purchaser the protection of the covenant in return for a substantial cash contribution to cover the estimated cost of remediation on the site. If the EPA does provide a covenant not to sue, it will require reopener clauses and local recording similar to those required for a *de minimis* settlement.

3.2.5 Right to Contribution

In the event a party is unable to avoid liability using the defenses discussed above, the responsible party may seek contribution from other responsible parties, including past property owners. SARA amendments to CERCLA specifically recognize a right of contribution among responsible parties by providing that:[31]

> Any person may seek contribution from any other person who is liable or potentially liable [under CERCLA] during or following any civil action. . . In resolving contribution claims, the court may allocate response costs among liable parties using such equitable factors as the court determines are appropriate.

While this section does not allow a party to escape liability, it does provide a mechanism whereby a party may reduce liability to the extent possible. For example, the purchaser of real estate who did not satisfy the "due diligence" requirements at the time of acquisition may be able to obtain contribution from prior owners who caused the contamination.

3.2.6 Private Actions

CERCLA also authorizes any person who may be liable under CERCLA to bring a private action seeking recovery of necessary costs of response incurred that are consistent with the National Contingency Plan.[32] Once a party incurs some response costs, that party may maintain a declaratory judgment action against other responsible parties for future response costs. Further, an administrative enforcement action by the EPA is not required as a prerequisite to maintaining a private action.[33]

Finally, CERCLA, as amended by SARA, specifically provides for the enforcement of indemnification agreements between private parties.[34] Although private indemnification agreements cannot be used by a party, otherwise liable to the government, to transfer that liability to another person, this section provides that the agreement will be enforceable between the private parties.

3.3 DEFENSES TO OTHER ENVIRONMENTAL REGULATIONS

The majority of the remaining environmental regulations frequently encountered in the transactional context are implemented through permit, operational, reporting, and recordkeeping requirements. As a result, the best defense available to avoid acquiring potential liability resulting from past activities of others when purchasing a facility, stock, or assets is to review the past permit compliance and reporting history of the entity being acquired. In addition, commercial lenders should review a borrower's compliance status prior to extending the loan.

To provide protection to the buyer and lender from these liabilities, the entity being acquired must first be analyzed to determine *all* permit, operational, reporting, and recordkeeping requirements of both present *and* past activities. Once determined, the compliance history of these activities must be researched to determine if any deviations from regulatory requirements have occurred. Each deviation represents a potential for future regulatory penalties. The magnitude of these deviations, when they occurred, and the enforcement history of the applicable regulatory agency must then be evaluated to determine the likelihood of those violations resulting in an actual penalty.

Depending on the severity of the violations, it may be necessary to approach the applicable agency in an attempt to enter into an agreement defining the penalty. While this activity may result in a penalty where one would not otherwise have been imposed, it will remove an element of risk from the transaction. Obviously, the approach to be taken must be decided on a case-by-case basis and be mutually agreed upon by the buyer, seller, and lender.

3.4 CONCLUSION

This chapter points out the importance of conducting an environmental site assessment of all property prior to acquisition. The assessment will advise the prospective purchaser and lender of any substantive problems regarding the present status and compliance history of the property and operations. The assessment is also a key element in satisfying the requirements of the statutory defenses and settlement provisions available to the innocent landowner should unanticipated problems arise in the future.

In the event liability to the government cannot be avoided, CERCLA provides private actions that may be used by an innocent purchaser to recover costs from prior owners or other responsible parties. These actions include contribution, private suit, or enforcement of indemnifications provided by separate agreement.

The second aspect of the assessment, particularly if the acquisition involves an on-going operation, is to determine if activities conducted on the site may subject the new owner to future penalties for past violations. Determination of the operation's compliance history will also provide the prospective purchaser with insights as to future operational problems and provide lenders with information to evaluate its risks.

The following chapter discusses the necessary elements of a site assessment. In addition, the chapter will address considerations in contracting for a site assessment.

REFERENCES

1. United States Code, Vol. 42, Sec. 9607.
2. *United States v. Monsanto Co.*, 858 F.2d 160 (4th Cir. 1988); *United States v. Chem-Dyne Corp.*, 572 F.Supp. 802 (S.D.Ohio 1983).
3. *Tanglewood East Homeowners' Assn. v. Charles Thomas, Inc.*, 849 F.2d 1568 (5th Cir. 1988).
4. United States Code, Vol. 42, Sec. 9607.
5. *United States v. Stringfellow*, 661 F.Supp. 1053 (C.D.Cal. 1987).
6. United States Code, Vol. 42, Sec. 9607.
7. *United States v. Northernaire Plating Co.*, 670 F.Supp. 742 (W.D.Mich. 1987).
8. *New York v. Shore Realty Corp.*, 759 F.2d 1032 (2d Cir. 1985).
9. Reich, E. and J. Cannon, "Guidance on Landowner Liability under Section 107(a)(1) of CERCLA, *De Minimis* Settlements under Section 122(g)(1)(B) of CERCLA, and Settlements with Prospective Purchasers of Contaminated Property," United States Environmental Protection Agency (June 6, 1989). (Hereinafter "EPA Guidance, June 6, 1989.")
10. *United States v. Hooker Chemicals & Plastics Corp.*, 680 F.Supp. 546 (W.D.N.Y. 1988).
11. United States Code, Vol. 42, Sec. 9601(35).
12. *Id.*
13. "Superfund Program; *De Minimis* Landowner Settlements, Prospective Purchaser Settlements," *Fed. Regist.* 54(159) (August 18, 1989).

14. "Conference Report on SARA," H.R. 2005, 99th Cong., 2d Sess., p. 187.
15. *Id.*
16. *United States v. Serafini,* 28 Env. Rep. Cas. 1162 (M.D.Pa. Feb. 19, 1988).
17. EPA Guidance, June 6, 1989, *supra.*
18. United States Code, Vol. 42, Sec. 9601(20)(A).
19. *United States v. Maryland Bank & Trust Company,* 632 F.Supp. 573 (D. Md. 1986); *United States v. Mirabile,* 15 E.L.R. 20992 (E.D.Pa. 1985).
20. United States Code, Vol. 42, Sec. 9601(35)(A)(iii).
21. "Conference Report on SARA," *supra.*
22. *United States v. Serafini,* 28 Env. Rep. Cas. 1162 (M.D.Pa. Feb. 19, 1988).
23. *PVO International Inc. v. Drew Chemical Corp.,* 19 E.L.R. 20077 (D.N.J. 1988).
24. *In Re Sterling Steel Treating, Inc. v. Becker,* 94 BANKR. 924 (E.D.Mich. 1989).
25. *BCW Associates, Ltd. v. Occidental Chemical Corp.,* 1988 W.L. 102641 (E.D.Pa. 1988) (unreported).
26. United States Code, Vol. 42, Sec. 9622(g).
27. EPA Guidance, June 6, 1989, *supra.*
28. *Id.*
29. *Id.*
30. *Id.*
31. United States Code, Vol. 42, Sec. 9613(f).
32. United States Code, Vol. 42, Sec. 9607(a).
33. *Wickland Oil Terminals v. Asarco, Inc.,* 792 F.2d 887 (9th Cir. 1986).
34. United States Code, Vol. 42, Sec. 9607(e).

CHAPTER **4**

Environmental Site Assessments

CHAPTER CONTENTS

Environmental Site Assessments

4.1 INTRODUCTION

In the previous chapter, the reader was advised of the limited statutory defenses to environmental liability available to purchasers or lenders. To qualify for these defenses, appropriate inquiry must be conducted prior to acquiring property. At a minimum, appropriate inquiry should consist of the following:

1. investigating current and previous owners and uses of the property;
2. inspection of the land and buildings on the property; and
3. contacting environmental agencies to determine if there is any known or suspected contamination or compliance problems at the site.

Other activities may also be necessary depending on the circumstances surrounding the transaction and the type of property that is involved. These investigative activities make up what is commonly referred to as the environmental site assessment (or simply site assessment).

The purpose of the environmental site assessment is to determine if there are any actual or potential environmental liabilities related to the property that may be passed on to subsequent users of the property. Environmental liabilities may result from numerous sources including the following:

1. contamination of property from past or current owners;
2. failure to comply with environmental regulations and permits by current or past owners; and
3. off-site contamination by wastes generated on-site (e.g., off-site disposal in a landfill).

The site assessment should investigate all of these potential sources of environmental liability and determine the nature and extent of any liabilities that are found.

Activities conducted as part of the site assessment can be grouped into three phases. The first phase, Phase I, includes those initial investigations to determine if there are any actual or suspected environmental liabilities at or related to the site. Phase I primarily consists of a review of documents (including the title search), inspection of the site, interviews with site personnel, and contacting environmental regulatory agencies for information on the site.

The second phase, Phase II, investigates any actual or potential liabilities that were identified during Phase I in order to ascertain the nature and extent of these liabilities. Activities conducted under Phase II include sampling and analysis of soils and ground- and surface waters, soil borings and soil gas surveys, underground storage tank testing, and any other surveys deemed necessary.

The final phase, Phase III, consists of investigation of remedial action alternatives for the site and commencement of remedial actions. This third phase is needed when contamination is present and must be addressed.

The focus of this chapter is on the first two phases only. Phase III activities are generally not required to meet the due diligence and appropriate inquiry requirements discussed in Chapter 3. There are numerous EPA documents, private publications, and articles on the subject of remedial actions.

This chapter is divided into four sections. The first section is an introduction. The second section provides a detailed discussion of the scope of environmental site assessments including:

1.   factors that affect the scope of the assessment;
2.   typical activities conducted under the assessment;
3.   follow-up activities that may need to be completed; and
4.   additional activities that could be conducted as part of the assessment.

The third section covers preparation of the site assessment report and the types of information to be provided in the report. The last section provides considerations involved in contracting for an assessment including who, how, and when to contract for an assessment and estimated costs for conducting a site assessment.

4.2 SCOPE OF AN ENVIRONMENTAL SITE ASSESSMENT

4.2.1 Factors Affecting the Scope of a Site Assessment

The initial activities to be conducted for an environmental site assessment will vary depending on a number of factors including the following:

1.   current and past uses of the property;
2.   current and past owners of the property;
3.   proposed use of the property;
4.   current and past uses of surrounding properties; and
5.   purposes of the site assessment.

The current and past uses of the site known by the principals to the transaction will probably be the determining factors dictating the initial scope of the assessment. The following questions must be answered in the early stages of the assessment:

1. Is the site undeveloped and/or dominated by mature vegetation?
2. How large is the site and are there any buildings on the site?
3. How old are the buildings on the site?
4. What were the past uses of those buildings?
5. Is the site or the surrounding area served by private or public water or sewer services?
6. Did any operations, past or present, handle or generate hazardous materials?
7. Have underground tanks ever been located on the property?
8. Are there any areas of known contamination on the property?
9. Were any operations, past or present, subject to environmental regulation?
10. Are there any known regulatory violations?

The future uses of the site may also affect the scope of the assessment. These considerations include:

1. Will future uses be residential, commercial, or industrial?
2. Will there be significant grading or excavation on the site?
3. Will current operations be expanded? Will groundwater be used by future operations?

The location of the property and the types of properties in the immediate area may also affect the assessment. These considerations include:

1. Is the area rural, residential, commercial, or industrial?
2. Is the area prone to floods, earthquakes, tornadoes, or hurricanes?
3. Is the groundwater or adjacent surface water a drinking water source?
4. Is there a hazardous waste site in the area?
5. Do any neighboring properties have underground storage tanks or other potential sources of contamination?
6. Are there schools, wildlife refuges, parks, or other properties in the area considered to be "sensitive"?

Finally, who the principals involved in the transaction are and their requirements for the site assessment will affect the scope of the assessment.

1. Is the property proposed for immediate development?
2. Is the buyer an individual, corporation, or other entity?
3. Is the assessment required by or will it be relied upon by a lender?

The answers to these questions will help in determining the initial scope of the assessment and consequently the activities that need to be conducted and the estimated cost for these activities. As additional information is gathered, the initial scope of the assessment may need to be expanded if actual or suspected environmental liability is discovered.

To obtain answers to the questions listed above, a questionnaire and disclosure statement should be submitted to the seller to complete prior to the assessment. If any parts of the completed statement are incomplete or vague, the seller (or the seller's representatives) should be contacted to clarify the required information.

4.2.2 Basic Site Assessment Activities — Phase I

The purpose of Phase I of the site assessment is to determine if there are any actual or suspected environmental liabilities at or related to the site. There are essentially three main elements of Phase I:

1. title search and review of related documents;
2. inspection of the property and interviews with persons connected with the site; and
3. contacting applicable environmental regulatory agencies for information on the property.

These activities are described in detail below.

4.2.2.1 Title Search and Review of Documents Related to the Site

The first element of the site assessment includes conducting a title search and reviewing related documents. The records of the property, usually available at the city or county land records office, need to be examined to determine all previous owners of the property of record. The chain of title will give the names of previous owners, which may provide information as to previous uses of the property. The records may also identify long-term lessees who may have occupied the property.

This information is important in evaluating whether or not past activities on the site may have resulted in contamination of the property. Furthermore, any special covenants or restrictions on use of the property as well as notices of contamination in the deed should also be identified.

In addition to title records, there are many other public sources of information that can be reviewed to obtain information on the site. Aerial photographs of the site and neighboring sites should also be examined, if available. Aerial photographs can reveal past uses of the sites such as the presence of buildings, lagoons, or tanks.

Appropriate federal, state, and local authorities should be contacted to identify known or suspected hazardous waste sites on the property and neighboring properties. The EPA, most states, and many local agencies maintain lists of hazardous waste sites. The initial list to be consulted is the National Priorities List (NPL), which includes sites that have scored in excess of 28.5 on EPA's Hazard Ranking System. These sites are known to be contaminated.

The EPA also maintains a secondary list, known as the CERCLIS (CER-

CLA Information System) list, which provides a comprehensive listing of suspected hazardous waste sites. CERCLIS is maintained by U.S. Post Office zip code boundaries and contains many sites not listed on the NPL. It is important to note that many of these sites are listed only because they have not yet been investigated by the EPA. Finally, many states and local governments maintain lists parallel to the federal lists.

If the property to be acquired is owned by a corporation, the corporation's annual report should be reviewed. Corporations whose stock is publicly traded are required to prepare annual 10K reports and quarterly 10-Q reports that present general and financial information on the corporation. The Securities Exchange Commission (SEC) requires such corporations to divulge in these reports any significant environmental legal actions against the corporation and potential financially significant environmental liabilities.

Other documentation that may also be helpful include tax records, water and sewer billing records, zoning records, old newspapers, and historical society records.

4.2.2.2 Inspection of the Property and Interviews of Site Personnel

The second and most important element of the site assessment consists of inspection of the property and interviews of persons with knowledge of the site. Inspection of the property consists of the following activities:

1. inspecting land and any surface water present on the subject and surrounding properties;
2. inspection of any existing facilities on the property;
3. investigating the operations of the property; and
4. reviewing company records, including permits, annual waste generation reports, compliance reports, manifests, site plans, etc.

Inspection of the land and surface water involves visually examining the soils and water for signs of contamination. These signs could include such obvious items as leaking drums, chemical residues, or waste pits. Less obvious signs could include soil discoloration, chemical odors, stunted vegetation, or an oily sheen on a pond or pool of rainwater.

Inspection of the facilities on the property would also include looking for similar signs of contamination, but would go further by actually looking for actual or potential sources of contamination. Such sources could include wastewater discharge pipes, drums, tanks, transformers, etc.

Inspection of the facilities is generally done in conjunction with the auditing of any operations on the site. Such operations could include manufacturing, warehousing, trucking, waste treatment, or disposal. Auditing of operations is a common environmental compliance activity conducted by in-house personnel or outside consultants to evaluate the company's compliance with environmental regulations. These audits look for potential liabilities and recommend solutions for any observed problems. The audit conducted as part of the site assessment generally performs the same functions with less emphasis on solutions and more emphasis on the potential costs of correcting any observed problems.

A detailed discussion of environmental audits is beyond the scope of this book. Numerous articles and books have been written on the subject, some of which are contained in the list of references at the end of this chapter.

The facility audit should identify the type and quantity of all hazardous materials handled or stored at the site. All areas of the site where hazardous materials are present, including manufacturing operations, material storage and handling areas, and maintenance shops, should be examined to evaluate the potential for release of these materials to the environment.

The audit should also identify all wastes and waste streams generated by the facility including the following:

1. hazardous waste;
2. solid waste (to determine if it may actually be hazardous);
3. wastewater; and
4. air pollutants.

Inspection of industrial operations should also consist of evaluating safety hazards with respect to employees, visitors, and the surrounding community. As in the case of environmental liability, safety violations and hazards can lead to lawsuits, fines, and required facility modifications. Any apparent safety hazards should be identified in the site assessment report.

The audit should also review the facility's environmental records and documents to look for potential environmental liabilities. Such liabilities could include the following:

1. violations of wastewater discharge or air emission standards;
2. inadequate or missing procedural documents required by RCRA, CERCLA, and CWA;
3. shipment of wastes off-site to disposal facilities which may be subject to Superfund cleanup requirements; and
4. documentation of releases (such as leaks and spills) and any response actions.

Most professionals conducting site assessments use some sort of checklist to inspect and evaluate a site. The checklist serves several purposes:

1. it provides the principals to the transaction with the issues to be evaluated during the assessment;
2. it ensures that all necessary issues are examined by the person(s) conducting the assessment; and
3. it provides for documentation of all issues.

An outline of the checklist developed by the authors is provided in Appendix

B. This outline is provided for illustrative purposes and presents the major areas of the checklist that is typically used during an assessment. The complete checklist containing detailed items to be evaluated is modified for each site based on information obtained from the questionnaire and disclosure statement prepared by the seller. For example, if it can be confirmed that the facility does not have any treatment systems or underground storage tanks (USTs), then these sections of the checklist may be removed prior to visiting the site.

The last activity conducted under property inspection is identifying neighboring properties and their uses. The purpose of this activity is to determine if there may be environmentally sensitive or damaging properties that could be affected by, or adversely affect, the site being assessed.

The presence of environmentally sensitive areas adjacent to the site may necessitate stricter environmental standards for facility operations and cleanup standards. Examples of environmentally sensitive areas include wetlands, parks, wildlife refuges, schools, or residential areas.

Environmentally damaging properties in the area could contaminate the site. Examples of possible environmentally damaging areas include waste sites, landfills, and manufacturing or warehousing facilities storing hazardous materials.

In addition to inspection of the property, this second element of the site assessment includes interviewing persons with knowledge of the site. For an active site (e.g., industrial or commercial operations on the site), the obvious people to contact and interview would be the people working at the site. Generally, it is advisable to interview the facility or operations manager, maintenance person, and any other employees that have been working at the site for a number of years and would have been involved with operations that could have caused environmental problems.

Prior to interviewing company employees, however, the consultant must be advised as to the employee's knowledge of the transaction. In most cases, the assessment is performed in the early stages of the transaction. Because the transaction is not yet a certainty, management has usually not yet announced the possibility of a sale to the employees. If this is the case, the consultant must be cautious not to disclose this information to the employees prematurely.

Information obtained from company personnel must also be taken in the appropriate context. Company personnel in upper management may stand to realize profits if the transaction is completed. As a result, they may attempt to "gloss over" problems at the facility. Lower level employees may also be reluctant to disclose information on potential problems for fear of reprisals from management or the possibility of an enforcement action closing down operations indefinitely.

Conversely, if there are tensions between labor and management, some employees may actually fabricate potential problems in order to cause problems for management. Thus, while employee interviews are extremely important in evaluating the status of the plant, the accuracy of that information should be confirmed by independent analysis.

Where the site is inactive but formerly was active, former employees as described above should be sought and interviewed. Where former employees cannot be identified or where the site is undeveloped, other persons may need to be contacted to tap their knowledge of the site and former activities. Such persons could include:

1. neighbors who lived in the area during past activities;
2. local police and fire departments;
3. local sewer and health departments; and
4. previous owners of the property.

4.2.2.3 Contacting Environmental Regulatory Agencies

The third element of any site assessment involves contacting applicable environmental regulatory agencies to obtain available information on the site. The information sought should include identification of all violations, fines, penalties, or pending actions against the owners or operators of the site and any knowledge of contamination at or near the site.

Inquiry should also be made as to any environmental permits issued to the operations on the property. Copies of inspection reports, waste manifests, annual waste summaries, or discharge monitoring reports are also helpful in evaluating the company's compliance history.

It is likely there will be more than one agency responsible for conducting regulatory activities for a particular environmental area (such as water, air, or hazardous waste). For example, the local sewerage treatment authority may be approved to regulate discharge of wastewater to its sanitary sewer in compliance with the Federal Pretreatment Regulations, but the state may, and the EPA does, have regulatory oversight authority to ensure that the local authority properly implements these requirements.

The extent of agency contact, as well as which party initiates this contact, must be worked out between the buyer and seller and conveyed to the consultant conducting the assessment. The considerations in reaching this agreement are discussed in Chapter 6.

Most federal and state agencies must make information available to the public under federal and state freedom of information laws. Many agencies have a designated freedom of information officer who is responsible for processing these requests. Generally, information requests will have to be made in writing and responded to by the agency in writing, and typically take up to two months. In some cases, phone calls or visits to the agencies' regulatory staffs may expedite obtaining the requested information.

4.2.3 Follow-Up Site Assessment Activities — Phase II

After completion of the basic site assessment activities described above, the results of these activities are examined and evaluated. If any actual or suspected contamination was found but the nature and extent of the contamination is not fully known, further investigation is needed. The purpose of the Phase II investigation is to more fully define the potential problems on the site, including type, location, and extent of contamination existing on the site.

Phase II follow-up activities generally include the following:

1. soil borings and/or soil gas survey;
2. soil sampling and analysis;
3. surface water sampling and analysis;
4. groundwater sampling and analysis;
5. metal detection surveys (to locate buried drums, tanks);
6. seismic, electrical, and electromagnetic surveys (to define subsurface geologic and hydrologic conditions);
7. underground storage tank testing; and
8. investigating and interviewing additional persons with knowledge of the site.

Examples of follow-up activities for potential sources of liability are listed in Table 4-1. The information in this table illustrates some typical activities conducted to investigate and evaluate areas at the site that could be contaminated as well as off-site liabilities.

4.2.4 Additional Site Assessment Activities

There are additional activities that can be conducted as part of the site assessment. These activities would be conducted because:

1. they are recommended by the consultant or environmental counsel as a prerequisite to providing environmental opinion;
2. they are required by the client or related party to the transaction as a prerequisite to closing; or
3. Phase II study indicates presence of contamination and potential liability.

Some of these additional activities are described below.

Where Phase I activities have identified potential liabilities for off-site disposal of wastes, investigations of transporters and treatment, storage, and disposal (TSD) facilities used by the company should be conducted. These investigations are important for determining if any contractors handling, transporting, or disposing of the subject company's hazardous wastes are liable for cleanup of any releases or environmental contamination. In addition, such investigations should examine the potential for future liability for disposing of the subject company's wastes.

Landfills and surface impoundments that are or could be designated Superfund sites subject to cleanup are of particular concern. Because of CERCLA's provisions for collection of cleanup costs from any entity which produced waste deposited at the site, i.e., generators, off-site liability could be imposed on successive owners regardless of fault.

Table 4-1.   Follow-Up Activities for Investigating Potential Sources of Liability

Potential Source of Liability	Follow-Up Activities
Underground storage tanks	Tank integrity tests, leak detection, subsurface sampling, removal of tanks
Material handling areas	Look for evidence of spills such as discoloration or odors; conduct surface sampling
Evidence of fill areas	Subsurface sampling, magnetometer survey; interview site personnel and neighbors, review aerial photographs and old topographical maps
Waste drums evident	Sample material in drums, if any; soil/subsurface sampling
Floor drains present in hazardous materials handling areas	Evaluate potential for release to drain; determine discharge point of drain
Pond, rivers, or lagoon on site	Sample water or sediments if contamination suspected
Electrical transformers	Examine for labels and leaks, review records, sample dielectric fluid and any discolored soils for PCBs
Off-site shipments of hazardous waste	Review manifests to identify treatment/disposal facility; investigate off-site facility to determine potential liability

Investigation of the waste transporters and waste management facilities would begin by analyzing company manifests (typically done as part of Phase I of the assessment) to determine the ultimate disposition of wastes generated by the company. Contact would then be made with the applicable companies and regulatory agencies to determine if environmental problems are present, particularly if the site has been designated for cleanup under CERCLA. Waste sites would also be compared against the federal National Priorities List (NPL) and state hazardous waste sites lists. Follow-up on-site audits of these companies' facilities may also be needed.

Another activity is evaluation of actions required to remediate potential environmental liabilities at the site. Depending on the client's needs, the results of the assessment can be used to estimate these costs. For example, if underground storage tanks are discovered, the costs of remediation may include removing the contents of the tank, investigating the extent of contamination, if any, and disposal of contaminated soil. Analysis of any required actions and costs may be necessary to allow the parties to determine how the original terms of the transaction may be adjusted to incorporate the findings of the site assessment.

4.3 SITE ASSESSMENT REPORT

Once the site assessment activities have been completed, a report can be prepared detailing the findings and recommendations of the assessment. The format and contents of the report will vary depending on the transaction, site, and consultants preparing the report. However, the report should contain the following:

1. scope and intent of assessment;
2. brief description of site;
3. results of title search;
4. results of aerial photography analysis;
5. description of past and present uses;
6. results of review of other documents;
7. results of property inspection;
8. results of employee interviews;
9. results of contacts with regulatory agencies;
10. list of applicable environmental permits with compliance history;
11. results of any other activities conducted on the site;
12. list of all information reviewed during the assessment;
13. summary of any potential problems; and
14. recommendations where necessary.

The site assessment report will not make definite conclusions regarding liability at the property other than stating the findings as determined by the assessment. Most reputable environmental consultants will not certify a property to be free of contamination or liability or guess at the extent of contamination without appropriate analyses. However, the report should present a basis for the prospective buyer or lender to make an informed decision as to whether to proceed or cancel the transaction.

In addition, in the event subsequent contamination is encountered on the site, the report will provide evidence that appropriate inquiry was conducted prior to the transaction. This may allow the purchaser to qualify for the innocent purchaser defense or a *de minimis* settlement as described in Chapter 3.

The consultant conducting the assessment should discuss the results of the assessment with the key principals involved in this transaction to explain the report's findings and recommendations. For further discussions on understanding the results of the site assessment, see Chapter 5.

4.4 CONTRACTING FOR THE SITE ASSESSMENT

4.4.1 Who to Contract for the Assessment

Once you have decided that an environmental site assessment is needed to protect you or your client's interests in a pending property acquisition, what's next?

First you must decide who will do the assessment. Only qualified and experienced environmental professionals should be used to perform the work. Prior experience and references are important, as well as professional certifications (e.g., licensed professional engineer, certified professional geologist, etc.).

When determining the consultant to be used, it is helpful to know something about the site. If the site has industrial operations, the consultant should have experience with conducting environmental audits of such operations and familiarity with the applicable environmental regulations and implementing agencies. If the site has known contamination of the soil that may impact the groundwater, then the consultant should have hydrogeologic experience. In addition, an attorney or title search specialist should also be on the assessment team to conduct the appropriate review of local legal records.

In some cases it may be advantageous for the site assessment consultant to be contracted through a law firm, thus allowing the results of the site assessment to be kept confidential pursuant to the attorney-client privilege. This privilege, however, may be penetrated under certain circumstances. For example, if the site assessment determines that a release of hazardous materials in excess of reportable quantities under CERCLA or other regulatory requirements has occurred, such information must be disclosed to the appropriate regulatory agency.

4.4.2 How to Contract for the Assessment

When contracting for the assessment, the consultant and client should detail the activities to be conducted under the initial assessment in the contract scope of work. The consultant should also be provided a copy of the contract of sale. As will be discussed in Chapter 6, the contract will often define the authorized activities that may be conducted by the purchaser or his agents. This could control the consultant's ability to inspect the site, interview company personnel, and contact regulatory agencies. The consultant needs this information to design the scope of the assessment, as well as provide an accurate estimate of the cost of the assessment.

After the appropriate scope of work has been determined, the consultant should also provide the estimated cost to perform these activities. This cost should also include preparation of a final report setting forth the consultant's findings.

Many consultants attempt to perform assessments under a lump sum contract. While many clients also prefer this type of contractual relationship, a time and expense contract offers certain advantages described below.

For the Phase I portion of the assessment, which involves significant document searches, a lump sum contract may cause the consultant to be less thorough in his review. Because of the potential liability associated with any omission of key information, it is usually preferable to compensate the consultant on a time and expense basis with an upper ceiling that cannot be exceeded without approval of the client. While this may give the consultant an open door, the consultant must stay within the scope of work provided in the contract. This type of contract usually provides the consultant enough flexibility to thoroughly complete the assessment, and also provides the client a cap on the cost of the assessment. Further, any additional work deemed necessary during the course of the assessment may easily be provided for by appropriate change order.

4.4.3 When to Contract for the Assessment

The environmental site assessment should be conducted as early as possible in the property transfer or financing process. A site assessment can usually be conducted within a few days, but some results of the assessment (e.g., analytical results, written responses from regulatory agencies, etc.) can take 30 days or longer. Furthermore, preparation time of two to five days is normally needed to obtain necessary materials and information and put together the appropriate site assessment team to properly conduct the site assessment.

4.4.4 How Much Will the Assessment Cost

The cost of an environmental site assessment is dependent on the activities conducted under the site assessment, which are dependent on the circumstances of the transaction and the site. Because the cost of the assessment is so variable, only estimates of costs and professional hourly rates are provided to give the reader an idea of anticipated costs

The average cost of an environmental site assessment is generally between $3500 and $5000. This price would cover the cost of Phase I of the assessment of a small site with no sampling and analytical costs.

The cost of an assessment would increase with increasing size of the site, number and size of buildings, operations with known hazardous materials, and known environmental contamination. Obviously, follow-up and optional activities will also increase the cost of the assessment.

Labor rates for experienced environmental professionals will generally range from $75 to $150 per hour. Rates for sampling technicians range from $25 to $50 per hour.

Analytical costs for metals will cost $15 to $30 per metal, per sample. Analysis of toxic organic pollutants is more expensive than metals and will vary depending on the pollutant. Generally, organic pollutants will be analyzed in groups for a single price. For example, analysis of volatile organic compounds will generally cost from $150 to $500. Bulk asbestos phase contrast microscopy analysis typically costs between $25 and $35 per sample.

Although the costs of conducting an environmental assessment may seem high, the costs of not conducting an assessment could be 100 to 1,000 times higher.

REFERENCES

1. "Real Estate Transactions and Environmental Law" (New York State Bar Association, 1987).
2. Hall, R. M., Jr., and D. R. Case. "All About Environmental Auditing" (Washington, DC: Federal Publications, Inc., 1987).
3. Cahill, L., and R. Kane. "Environmental Audits," 5th ed. (Rockville, MD: Government Institutes, March 1987).
4. "Superfund Exposure Assessment Manual," Office of Remedial Response, U.S. EPA Report-540/1-88/001 (April 1988).
5. "Guidance for Conducting Remedial Investigations and Feasibility Studies Under CERCLA, Interim Final," Office of Emergency and Remedial Response, U.S. EPA Report-540/G-89/004 (October 1988).

CHAPTER 5

Understanding the Results of an Environmental Site Assessment

CHAPTER CONTENTS

Understanding the Results of an Environmental Site Assessment

5.1 INTRODUCTION

The following scenario is likely to be encountered by the reader:

You are involved with the acquisition of an industrial property. You determine that an environmental site assessment is needed and contract a consultant to conduct the assessment and prepare a report. The report describes actual and suspected environmental violations and contamination found during the assessment. However, you are having difficulty understanding the report's findings and determining if and how to proceed with acquisition of the property.

The reason such a scenario is likely is that the layperson will not have the knowledge and references to understand and evaluate the results of the assessment. The purpose of this chapter is to provide the reader with a basic understanding of how to interpret the results of a site assessment report.

This chapter is divided into four sections. The first section is the introduction. The next section presents a compendium of environmental standards with which to compare analytical results of environmental contamination at the site. Some of these standards are regulatory requirements whereas others are guidelines to be used as appropriate for the circumstances of the site.

The third section then discusses the contents of a site assessment report and the potential problems that might be found during the site assessment. Examples of environmental liability, "red flags", that the reader should be on the alert for are also identified in this section. The last section presents a brief conclusion to this chapter and introduces the next chapter, which discusses applying the results of the site assessment to the transaction.

5.2 ENVIRONMENTAL STANDARDS

5.2.1 General

The environmental site assessment, in many cases, will require sampling and analysis of soils and surface or groundwater. The analytical results will list the pollutants tested for and the concentration of pollutants found on the site.

The pollutants that are present and their concentrations will dictate if remedial actions need to be taken. Such actions could include reducing concentrations of the pollutants through treatment, containing the contamination, or removing the contaminated soils or water for off-site treatment or disposal. If pollutants are present in significant concentrations it will be readily apparent that remedial actions are needed. However, if pollutants are present at low levels, it is difficult to determine if the low-level contamination poses a potential environmental hazard.

This section presents various environmental standards that may be appropriate to evaluate site assessment analytical results. These standards should be used only as guidelines until applicable standards are determined by the appropriate regulatory agencies.

It is important to note that one set of standards may apply to one site or even to one type of media at a site and another set of standards would apply to another site or media. Consequently it is necessary to check with federal, state, or local officials on applicable environmental standards for each contaminated media for each site. For disposal of contaminated materials off-site, the treatment/disposal facility will set their own standards for accepting the wastes.

5.2.2 SARA ARARs

Prior to the passage of the 1986 Superfund Amendments and Reauthorization Act (SARA), cleanup standards for waste disposal sites were not specified by the Comprehensive Environmental Response Compensation and Liability Act (CERCLA). Consequently, it was difficult for persons responsible for remedial actions at a site to determine what standards needed to be attained, i.e., "how clean is clean." SARA attempts to set cleanup standards by specifying that remedial actions at waste disposal sites must at least attain applicable or relevant and appropriate requirements (ARARs). "Applicable requirements" and "relevant and appropriate requirements" are defined in the proposed National Contingency Plan, 53 Federal Register 51435, December 21, 1988 as follows:

> "Applicable requirements means those cleanup standards, standards of control, and other substantive environmental protection requirements, criteria, or limitations promulgated under federal or state law that specifically address a hazardous substance, pollutant, contaminant, remedial action, location or other circumstance at a site.
>
> . . .
>
> "Relevant and appropriate requirements mean those cleanup standards (that)... address problems or situations sufficiently similar to those encountered at the CERCLA site that their use is well suited to the particular site."

The EPA ARARs policy fact sheet[1] explains these definitions as follows:

"In other words, an applicable requirement is one that a private party would have to comply with by law if the same action was being taken apart from CERCLA authority. All jurisdictional prerequisites of the requirement must be met in order for the requirement to be applicable. If a requirement is not applicable, it still may be relevant and appropriate. A requirement that is relevant and appropriate may 'miss' on one or more prerequisites but still make sense at the site, given the circumstances of the site and release."

Essentially the SARA ARARs policy requires analysis of all of the circumstances of contamination at the site, including proposed remedial actions, to determine the applicable or relevant and appropriate standards and criteria.

ARARs are standards to be applied in determining what levels need to be attained by remedial actions at a contaminated site. Although ARAR standards legally only apply to Superfund sites, they can be used as guidance in evaluating contamination at a non-Superfund site, such as would be the case for an environmental site assessment. For example, where Phase II assessment activities involving sampling and analysis have determined pollutant concentrations, the ARARs can be compared with the pollutant concentrations to evaluate the potential need for remediation at the site.

Further guidance on ARARs is contained in Parts I and II of the EPA "CERCLA Compliance With Other Laws Manual."[2,3] Exhibit 1-1 from the Manual, Part I (reprinted in part in Appendix C) lists potential ARARs for selected hazardous substances and pollutants. These potential ARARs are drawn from the Safe Drinking Water Act, the Resource Conservation and Recovery Act, and the Clean Water Act. These three kinds of ARARs are discussed below.

5.2.3 Drinking Water Standards

The Safe Drinking Water Act (SDWA) and accompanying regulations require public drinking water sources to meet certain maximum contaminant levels (MCLs). The EPA has promulgated MCLs for some pollutants, proposed revised standards for some of these pollutants, and proposed standards for additional pollutants. The existing and proposed MCLs are listed in Table 5-1.

Drinking water MCLs are used as cleanup standards in cases where contaminated groundwater or surface water is or could be used for drinking water. However, some regulatory agencies may require that the MCLs be used as standards for these waters even if it is not a drinking water source. A regulatory agency's ability to enforce such standards will depend on the relevant circumstances of the site.

Drinking water MCLs that are proposed but have not been promulgated are not enforceable. However, guidance from the EPA has indicated that the pre-

**Table 5-1.   Safe Drinking Water Act Maximum Contaminant Levels (MCLs)
January 1, 1990**

Contaminant	Existing MCL (mg/l)	Proposed MCL (mg/l)
Benzene	0.005	0.005
Carbon tetrachloride	0.005	0.005
1,2-Dichloroethane	0.005	0.005
Trichloroethylene	0.005	0.005
para-Dichlorobenzene	0.075	0.075
1,1-Dichloroethylene	0.007	0.007
1,1,1-Trichloroethane	0.2	0.2
Vinyl chloride	0.002	0.002
cis-1,2-Dichloroethylene	none	0.07
1,2-Dichloropropane	none	0.005
Ethylbenzene	none	0.7
Monochlorobenzene	none	0.1
ortho-Dichlorobenzene	none	0.6
Styrene	none	0.005/0.1
Tetrachloroethylene	none	0.005
Toluene	none	2
trans-1,2-Dichloroethylene	none	0.1
Xylenes (total)	none	10
Fluoride	2	4
Asbestos	none	7 mf/l
Barium	1.0	5
Cadmium	0.01	0.005
Chromium	0.05	0.1
Mercury	0.002	0.002
Nitrate	10 as N	10 as N
Nitrite	none	1 as N
Selenium	0.01	0.05
Alachlor	none	0.002
Aldicarb	none	0.01
Aldicarb sulfoxide	none	0.01
Aldicarb sulfone	none	0.04
Atrazine	none	0.003
Carbofuran	none	0.04
Chlordane	none	0.002
Dibromochloropropane	none	0.0002
2,4-D	0.1	0.07
Ethylene dibromide	none	0.00005
Heptachlor	none	0.0004
Heptachlor epoxide	none	0.0002
Lindane	0.0004	0.0002
Methoxychlor	0.1	0.4
Polychlorinated biphenyls	none	0.0005
Pentachlorophenol	none	0.2
Toxaphene	0.005	0.005
2,4,5-TP (Silvex)	0.01	0.05

ferred remedy for a site may need to be adjusted if the MCL being used as an ARAR changes and will not be met by the remedy being implemented.

To conclude this section, the following generalizations can be made:

1. If the pollutant concentrations in the groundwater or surface water are below MCLs, no action may be needed.
2. If the pollutant concentrations in the water exceed MCLs and the water is a drinking water source, it is likely that remedial actions will be required to attain the MCLs.
3. If the pollutant concentrations exceed MCLs but the water is not a drinking water source, negotiations with applicable agencies will be necessary to ascertain whether remedial actions are needed and what the cleanup standards will be.

If the source of contamination of the water is not removed or contained, there could be future increases of pollutant levels in the water. Consequently, if there is contamination of water, it is important to identify the source and determine if further contamination will occur. The potential for future contamination may require remedial actions despite acceptable levels of pollutants. Finally, it must be remembered that the agencies exercise broad discretion in determining cleanup standards, and this discretion is generally exercised very conservatively.

5.2.4 RCRA Hazardous Waste Standards

Resource Conservation and Recovery Act (RCRA) hazardous waste regulations define what is a hazardous waste. If a material is a hazardous waste pursuant to these regulations, then it must be stored, managed, transported, and disposed of as a hazardous waste according to the complex (and expensive) regulatory requirements under RCRA. There are two ways a material may be a hazardous waste: (1) if it exhibits the characteristics of a hazardous waste, i.e., corrosivity, ignitability, reactivity, or toxicity; and (2) if it is specifically listed in the regulations as a hazardous waste.

The regulations defining what is a hazardous waste are contained in Part 261 of Title 40 of the Code of Federal Regulations. These standards as they relate to ARARs are also included in Appendix C.

With regard to potential liability for contamination at a site, RCRA standards will usually apply only where soils are highly contaminated or hazardous wastes are present on the site (such as in drums, tanks, landfills, or surface impoundments) and need to be disposed of off-site. Sampling and analysis of soils and wastes on the site conducted as part of the assessment will determine what soils and wastes may be hazardous and subject to RCRA regulations. Off-site disposal of materials identified as hazardous wastes will likely subject the property owner to significant disposal costs.

5.2.5 Water Quality Criteria

The EPA has developed recommended maximum levels for numerous pollutants for protection of human health and aquatic life in salt and freshwater bodies. These recommended maximum pollutant levels are known as water quality criteria and are listed in Appendix C.

The criteria for the protection of human health is based on the acceptable risk and toxicity of the pollutant entering the human body through ingestion of fish only and ingestion of fish and water. The criteria for the protection of aquatic life is based on toxicity studies using certain sensitive organisms that are indigenous to either salt or freshwater environments. The chronic toxicity criteria for aquatic life are designed to protect these organisms against long-term effects while acute toxicity criteria are designed to protect these organisms against short-term lethality.

Section 121 of CERCLA states that hazardous substances, pollutants, or contaminants left on-site at the conclusion of the remedial action shall attain federal water quality criteria where they are relevant and appropriate under the circumstances of the site. This section further states that this determination is to be based on the designated or potential use of the water, the media affected, the purposes of the criteria, and current information.

In other words, water quality criteria may apply under certain circumstances, notably where there is a surface water body on the site or drainage of ground or surface wastes goes to a surface water body. However, water quality criteria may be preempted by state water quality standards where such standards exist for the surface water body and by drinking water MCLs where the water may be a source of drinking water.

5.2.6 New Jersey Trigger Levels

The state of New Jersey is currently developing standards for a variety of pollutants to be used for evaluating property contamination. The standards are expected to be promulgated sometime in 1990. Until then, the New Jersey Department of Environmental Protection, Division of Hazardous Waste Management uses the pollutant criteria listed in Table 5-2 as guidelines. These criteria, sometimes referred to as "trigger levels," were developed by the Department as interim guidelines to help in determining when remedial actions are required at a contaminated site.

The criteria in the table are divided into two columns: trigger levels for pollutants in soils and for pollutants in groundwater. The state's policy is that if pollutant levels in soils or groundwater exceed the criteria, then it is likely that remedial actions will be needed at the site and further investigations must be conducted.

Because these criteria are only guidelines and only apply in the state of New Jersey, they are not regulatory standards. However, where standards do not exist, these trigger levels can be used as a reference for evaluating the contamination at a site and the need for remedial actions until standards are set by the applicable agency.

Table 5-2.   State of New Jersey Trigger Levels[a]

Contaminant	Soils (ppm)	Groundwater (ppb)
Total volatile organic compounds (VOCs)	1	10
Total base neutral extractable compounds	10	50
Total acid extractable compounds	10	50
Total petroleum hydrocarbons	100	1,000
PCBs	1-5	1
Cyanide	12	200
Antimony	10	none[b]
Arsenic	20	50
Barium	400	1,000
Beryllium	1	none[b]
Cadmium	3	10
Chromium	100	50
Copper	170	1,000
Lead	250-1,000	50
Mercury	1	2
Nickel	100	none[b]
Selenium	4	10
Silver	5	50
Thallium	5	none[b]
Vanadium	100	none[b]
Zinc	350	5,000

[a]Source: Balakrishman, 1989.[4]

[b]No level has been set for these contaminants.

5.2.7 CERCLA Reportable Quantities

Regulations promulgated under CERCLA require notification of releases of hazardous materials in quantities exceeding prescribed amounts, known as "reportable quantities" or "RQs". These RQs are set forth in Part 302 of Title 40 of the Code of Federal Regulations. The regulations require notification to the EPA of any release to the environment exceeding the RQ, including leaking tanks, surface impoundments, tank trucks, or rail cars.

The use of the RQs in evaluating a site assessment report will apply in determining if there has been or potentially could be a release exceeding the RQ. The site assessment should provide information on quantities of hazardous materials on-site that have or could be released and such quantities should be compared with applicable RQs.

5.2.8 Radon Action Level Guidelines

Radon is a radioactive gas produced by the normal decay of radioactive materials found naturally in the ground. Such radioactive materials are widely distributed in trace amounts in soils throughout the U.S. and other parts of the world. Radon gas is colorless, odorless, and tasteless and thus undetectable without special measurement devices.

The presence of radon gas can significantly increase the risk of lung cancer. Radon gas generally enters buildings through cracks in foundation floors, sumps, and floor drains. The concentration of the gas will increase in buildings because of the restriction of air exchange to limit heat or air conditioning losses.

No federal or state regulations exist that set specific standards for radon in buildings. However, the EPA has issued guidelines for radon that specify levels requiring action to reduce radon. In an EPA publication,[6] four levels were identified and specific actions recommended. The radon level below which remedial actions are needed is 4 picocuries per liter of air (4 pCi/l). Radon concentrations below this level present relatively low risk and reductions below this level may be difficult. At the top end of the EPA's guidelines — that is, for radon concentrations that exceed 200 pCi/l — the EPA recommends taking remedial actions as soon as possible and even temporarily relocating persons in the building until levels are reduced. Remedial actions for reducing radon include sealing cracks in foundation floors, venting of sumps and floor drains, and increased air exchange in buildings.

Two final notes regarding radon: first, it is important that accurate testing results be obtained to make informed decisions on whether or not remedial actions are needed. EPA has surveyed various testing companies and methodologies and has identified several that do not give accurate results. Therefore, radon testing companies should be checked to ensure that they are approved by the EPA or state regulatory authorities prior to testing.

Second, radon testing is very site specific, that is, measurements of radon are only accurate for the immediate area being sampled. For example, radon may be found in a building or area of land but across the street in another building or 20 feet away from the first sampling area, radon may not be present. It is important that enough samples be taken to adequately evaluate the risk of radon.

5.3 POTENTIAL ENVIRONMENTAL LIABILITIES

5.3.1 General

The primary elements of the site assessment report (described in detail in Section 4.3) include the following:

1. brief description of the site and regulatory status;
2. findings of the title search and review of related documents;
3. findings of the inspection of the property, audit of the facilities on-site, and interviews with site personnel;
4. findings of any follow-up investigations; and
5. summary of potential environmental liabilities.

Assuming the environmental consultant conducting the assessment has done an effective job of investigating the potential environmental liabilities at the site, the report should identify all known environmental liabilities. There are numerous kinds of environmental liabilities that could be identified by the site assessment. Some liabilities require minimal cost to remedy and should not significantly affect the transaction. Others, however, could increase costs into the millions of dollars and could require significant restructuring or canceling the transaction. It is important that persons reading and relying on the results of the assessment report know what environmental liabilities may be found and the relative significance and potential costs of these liabilities.

To educate the reader on potential environmental liabilities, this section identifies examples of some common liabilities found during site assessments. The relative importance of each liability and the factors that would affect the costs of resolving the liability are also discussed.

The examples of potential environmental liabilities are grouped into the following three categories:

1. on-site contamination;
2. off-site contamination; and
3. environmental regulatory violations.

The first category covers liabilities from contamination at the site including contamination of soil, groundwater, surface water, buildings, and equipment. The second category includes liabilities for off-site contamination generally resulting from off-site disposal of hazardous wastes generated on the site. The third category covers liabilities that result from violation of environmental regulations by operations at the site.

5.3.2 On-Site Contamination

Example 1 — Underground Storage Tanks Identified On-Site
Most underground storage tanks (referred to as USTs) that contain chemicals and petroleum products are regulated under the Resource Conservation and Recovery Act (RCRA). These regulations cover notification, removal, installation, and leak detection requirements. State and local regulation of USTs are also common and need to be examined.

The identification of USTs is common when conducting site assessments. USTs are also one of the more frequent sources of contamination. If USTs are found at the site, it must be determined if these USTs are a likely source of contamination. This includes a determination of the age of the USTs, as well as what materials were stored in the USTs. The USTs should be tested to determine if they are leaking and/or the soil and groundwater surrounding the USTs tested for contamination.

If USTs are or were leaking hazardous materials (such as gasoline), then the tanks need to be removed and replaced (if the tanks are a necessary part of the operations at the site). Furthermore, any contamination resulting from the leaking tanks must be investigated and, in most cases, removed. The particular details of remedial investigations and actions will be dependent on the requirements of the state where the site is located.

The relative liability and associated costs of USTs at a site is dependent on the following:

1. number and age of the tanks;
2. contents of the tanks;
3. quantity of materials leaked from the tanks; and
4. type of soils and depth to groundwater in the area of the tanks.

A best-case scenario involving USTs would be where the tanks had not leaked and were emptied after discontinuation of their use. In such a case, the best action would be removal of the tanks, which would be relatively inexpensive (probably less than $10,000 per tank).

The other extreme would involve numerous older gasoline tanks (such as would exist at a closed gas station) where gasoline had leaked over a period of several years. Compounding this worst case would be a hydrogeological situation consisting of porous soils and groundwater used for drinking water. In this case, the cost of remediating the site, including investigating the extent of contamination and removing the gasoline from the soils and groundwater, could easily exceed hundreds of thousands of dollars.

Example 2 — Asbestos is Found in the Insulation
of the Office Building on the Site
Asbestos was commonly used in buildings built between the 1920s and the mid 1970s. Generally, asbestos is only hazardous when it is friable, i.e., in a state in which it can become airborne such as when asbestos-containing materials have been damaged or disturbed. Asbestos is regulated by federal and state laws. These laws regulate the renovation and demolition of buildings containing asbestos and set standards for asbestos in the air of such buildings. For example, the Occupational Safety and Health Administration (OSHA) has set a permissible exposure limit (PEL) of 0.2 fibers per cubic centimeter of air for workers engaged in asbestos remediation and disposal.

The federal law that requires removal of asbestos from buildings is the Asbestos Hazard Emergency Response Act of 1986 (AHERA). This law was passed as an amendment to the Toxic Substances Control Act (TSCA) and applies only to school buildings. Generally, asbestos does not have to be removed from other types of buildings unless asbestos is exposed and can be released into the air. However, it is anticipated that AHERA will be expanded in the future to cover all public and commercial buildings.

Many lenders express concerns regarding the presence of any asbestos, even nonfriable types. These lenders may require removal of asbestos because of the potential exposure to costly lawsuits from occupants.

In addition to regulatory concerns, the prospective buyer of a property should be concerned with the liability from past and future exposure of humans to asbestos in buildings. This liability stems from the potential for lawsuits from persons that were exposed and later developed diseases related to asbestos exposure.

Asbestos can be a significant liability, depending on the extent and state of the asbestos at the site. Remedial actions to reduce this liability include containment (generally referred to as encapsulation) or removal of asbestos. The cost of containment or removal of asbestos is dependent on the form and quantity of asbestos in a building, which is related to the type, age, and size of the building. Asbestos testing, air monitoring costs and potential for lawsuits from exposed persons must also be factored into the total cost of asbestos liability.

Example 3 — Transformers Containing PCBs are Present On-Site and Past Leaks of These Transformers Have Contaminated Soils

Polychlorinated biphenyls, commonly called PCBs, are regulated under TSCA. Regulations cover containment, removal, and disposal of PCBs. Regulations also address the inspection of transformers that contain PCBs and the necessary response to leaks from these transformers. PCBs are highly toxic and generally considered to be carcinogenic. PCBs are particularly insidious because of their tendency to bioaccumulate in animal and human tissue, as well as their resistance to degradation.

In this example, the transformers, if still in operation, can either be removed, treated to remove the PCBs, or sealed and inspected regularly to check for leaks. Depending on the quantity of PCBs spilled, the spill may also have to be reported to the appropriate federal and state officials. The contaminated soils must be removed and disposed of in an approved incinerator or landfill (depending on the concentration of PCBs).

EPA regulations provide specific policies regarding registration, inspection, reporting, and cleanup for transformers or other equipment containing PCBs. These activities must be conducted within timeframes provided by the regulations, and the owner must maintain specific records of the activities. Even if the facility is currently in compliance, the owner could still be liable for past failures to comply with these procedures.

It may be possible that the transformers on the site are owned by an electrical utility company. If so, the owner of the site should be able to recover the costs of any remedial investigations and cleanup from the utility company.

As in the previous examples, the potential cost of the liability from PCBs will be dependent on the number and size of the transformers on-site, the quantity of PCBs that have leaked, and the type and quantity of contaminated soils. To give an idea of the cost of disposal of PCBs, the disposal of a transformer containing PCBs can cost well over $10,000.

5.3.3 Off-Site Contamination

Example 4 — Hazardous Waste Generated by the Operations
Conducted on the Property was Buried in a Landfill That Has Been Designated
a Superfund Site

The cleanup of hazardous waste sites is covered under CERCLA (Superfund). Responsibility for cleanup of waste sites is imposed jointly and severally on the owner of the site, as well as the generators of the waste that was disposed at the site.

In this example, the company conducting the operations on the property to be acquired is most likely a potentially responsible party (PRP) in the investigation and cleanup of the disposal site. Under the CERCLA provisions for joint and several liability, the company could potentially be liable for the entire cost of cleanup. Practically speaking, however, the cost of cleanup to be assessed to the company will generally be dependent on the amount of waste contributed to the site, the number and financial strength of the other PRPs to the site, and the cost of cleanup of the site.

As a result of CERCLA's joint and several liability provision, the potential liability in this example may be quite extensive and costly. A typical Superfund cleanup involving a landfill could cost millions of dollars. Imposition of this type of off-site liability is generally limited to situations where the purchaser specifically assumes the seller's past liabilities or the assets were acquired through a corporate stock purchase. Consequently, this liability needs to be specifically addressed prior to acquisition.

Example 5 — Off-Site Contamination of Adjacent Property is Migrating onto
Property to be Acquired

Occasionally, the property to be acquired has been contaminated by activities conducted on an adjacent property. This frequently occurs when the subject property is located in an industrial park or adjacent to a property with underground storage tanks, such as a gas station. Contaminants released on these properties might enter the groundwater and migrate onto adjacent properties as part of natural groundwater flow patterns. Migration of contaminants may also occur by surface drainage flow patterns where the adjacent property is at higher elevations than the subject property.

The owner who acquires property that has been contaminated in this manner might still be liable as an "owner" under CERCLA. To avoid this liability, the new owner would have to establish the third party defense. This would require an affirmative showing that the contamination resulted from the acts or omissions of third parties with whom the purchaser had no contractual relationship. Thus, the owner of the site must prove that the on-site contamination was caused solely by activities on adjacent properties.

Depending on the history of on-site activities, the source of contamination may be difficult to prove. Therefore it is important that activities conducted on adjacent properties also be investigated as part of the site assessment.

5.3.4 Environmental Regulatory Violations

Example 6 — The Manufacturing Operations on the Site Have Continually Exceeded Wastewater Discharge Requirements Specified by the Local Sewer Authority

Requirements for the discharge of wastewater to sewerage systems (referred to as indirect discharges) are regulated under the Clean Water Act and by local ordinances. There are two primary costs to be concerned with in this example: (1) the cost of fines and penalties resulting from past and current violations and (2) the cost of correcting these violations through installation of a treatment system, process changes, or other means.

The cost of fines and penalties will be dependent on the types of violations, how long the violations have continued, and their effect on the sewage treatment plant (particularly with regard to the treatment plant meeting its direct discharge limits). Generally, the amounts of fines and penalties are difficult to predict. The Clean Water Act provides for penalties of up to $25,000 per violation per day. Although many local sewer authorities do not have authority to assess more than $1,000 per violation per day, if the EPA gets involved because of the type and duration of the violations, then the Act's higher penalties can be assessed. Further, in the absence of EPA enforcement, the operator could be subject to citizens' suits seeking significant penalties.

The cost of correcting the violations will be dependent on the types of violations and the discharge standards that need to be met. If the violations can be corrected through process, equipment or procedural changes, the costs may be relatively small. However, if treatment systems must be installed to reduce or eliminate pollutants, such systems could cost upwards of a million dollars or more depending on the type and size of the system needed.

The liability for past violations (including fines and penalties) would generally be imposed only where the purchaser specifically assumes the seller's past liabilities or the assets were acquired through a corporate stock purchase. However, the cost of correcting the violations (including process changes and/or treatment system installation) must be borne by the subsequent owner to ensure continued operation and limit future violations.

5.4 CONCLUSION

This chapter has given the reader some basic information, standards, and criteria with which to understand and evaluate the results of a site assessment. It is unlikely that a definitive determination can be made that a site has no environmental liability or, if environmental liability exists, the exact cost of the liability. Attempts to predict total exposure are further complicated when penalties are involved. However, the site assessment results, in conjunction with knowledge of the potential problems, environmental standards, and the costs of environmental liabilities, will allow the principals of the real estate transaction to make an informed decision as to how to proceed with the transaction.

The next chapter discusses what options are available to these principals to address the results of the assessment in the transaction and minimize liability.

REFERENCES

1.   "Superfund Fact Sheet ARARs Q's & A's," Office of Solid Waste and Emergency Response, U.S. EPA Pamphlet (May 1989).
2.   "CERCLA Compliance With Other Laws Manual: Draft Guidance," Office of Emergency and Remedial Response, U.S. Report-540/G-89/006 (August 1988).
3.   "CERCLA Compliance With Other Laws Manual: Part II," Office of Waste and Emergency Response, U.S. EPA Report-540/G-89/009 (August 1989).
4.   Balakrishman, S. New Jersey ECRA Group, Department of Environmental Protection. Personal Communication (November 1, 1989).
5.   Arbucklc, J. G., et al. "Environmental Law Handbook," 10th ed. (Rockville, MD: Government Institutes, March 1989).
6.   "A Citizens Guide to Radon," Office of Air and Radiation, U.S. EPA Report-OPA-86-004 (August 1986).
7.   "Radon Reduction Methods," Research and Development, U.S. EPA Report-OPA-86-005 (August 1986).
8.   "Radon/Radon Progeny Cumulative Proficiency Report," Office of Radiation Programs, U.S. EPA Report-520/1-86-008 (September 1986).

CHAPTER 6

Structuring the Transaction: Dealmaker v. Dealbreaker

CHAPTER CONTENTS

Structuring the Transaction: Dealmaker v. Dealbreaker

6.1 INTRODUCTION

Previous chapters have presented discussions of the potential environmental liabilities facing a prospective real estate purchaser. Included in these discussions have been the limited statutory defenses to liability provided by the laws that established this liability. Appropriate procedures have also been discussed that should be followed by the purchaser to satisfy the elements of these available defenses should liability be imposed in the future.

In today's market, the majority of environmental site assessments performed on industrial or commercial property will identify one or more potential sources of environmental concern. This chapter will lay out some alternatives available to the parties in the event environmental hazards are identified. It will also provide contract provisions that the buyer should seek to include in the contract of sale to provide protection in the event contamination is encountered on the site. A discussion of how the seller should seek to limit these provisions will conclude the chapter.

6.2 WHEN ENVIRONMENTAL ISSUES SHOULD BE ADDRESSED

Because of the complexity and potential magnitude of environmental liability, environmental issues must be addressed at the initiation of the transaction. Until recently, the environmental aspects of the transaction were typically not discussed until late in the transaction, if at all.

With the advent of cases like Shore Realty and Maryland Bank and Trust[1] (see Chapter 3), many lenders have required that environmental issues be addressed earlier in the negotiations. In order to prevent unanticipated surprises at closing, it is imperative that the scope of the environmental investigation be determined early in the negotiations. This means that environmental issues, including "kick-out clauses," warranties, representations, and indemnifications, should be addressed in the contract of sale or option. Further, the scope of the required environmental investigation, and associated opinion letter from counsel if required, must be clearly defined in the commitment letter between the lender and the borrower.

Delay in resolution of these issues will generally sacrifice negotiating position, increase the probability of delaying closing, and, most importantly, increase potential exposure to significant liability.

6.3 NEGOTIATION OF THE CONTRACT OF SALE

6.3.1 General Goals of the Parties

Prior to purchasing the property, the purchaser must determine as much as possible about past and current operations on the property. If this investigation indicates little likelihood of potential liability, the purchaser might qualify for one of the statutory defenses enumerated in earlier chapters. In the event the investigation determines that potential environmental hazards exist, the parties can use this information to either terminate the transaction or restructure the transaction to address these concerns. This section will suggest contract provisions frequently sought by the purchaser to provide flexibility to restructure the transaction should an environmental hazard be encountered during the course of the investigation. Also provided are limitations to these provisions frequently requested by the seller.

The prospective purchaser's concerns can essentially be grouped into two classes, the relative importance of which depends on the type of property or operation being acquired. The purchaser's initial concern is whether or not past activities on the site may have contaminated the site such that remediation may be required in the future. As indicated above, the new purchaser, as a present owner of the site, may be strictly liable for the entire cleanup of the site. If the subject property is undeveloped, this is typically the purchaser's overriding concern.

When the transaction involves an existing operation, the purchaser's second concern involves that operation's compliance history. The purchaser must investigate the compliance history of that operation to determine the potential for liability that may result from both past and future operations. A history of noncompliance not only represents a potential for penalties for past violations, but also indicates that potentially significant capital expenditures may be required in the future to prevent continued noncompliance. The contract of sale or option to purchase, whichever is applicable, must provide the purchaser the flexibility to address these concerns.

The interests of the lender should also be addressed early in the transaction. At the time of acquisition, the lender's interests are generally parallel to the purchaser's. The lender's main concern is protecting the property, which secures the transaction. Prior to the acquisition, the lender must be satisfied that no outstanding environmental liabilities exist. After closing, the lender will also be concerned that the operations are being properly conducted. As long as the property remains free of contamination, it remains available for foreclosure in the event of default. Lenders frequently provide for this protection by obtaining covenants from the borrower providing that the mortgaged property will not be used to store, treat, handle, or dispose of hazardous wastes. The scope of these covenants must be adequately adjusted, however, to allow the continuation of current activities on the site. Finally, in the event of default, the lender must once again exercise due diligence prior to acquiring title to the property through foreclosure.

The seller of industrial property is faced with conflicting interests in negotiating the sale of the property. In today's market, it is unrealistic to attempt to sell the property without allowing the purchaser to conduct an environmental assessment of the site. Previously unknown environmental concerns encountered by the assessment, however, may have to be disclosed to the applicable regulatory agency. This disclosure may subject the seller to significant liability that could exceed the value of the property. Often the buyer will seek to terminate the transaction, leaving the seller with newly discovered environmental liabilities.

Alternatively, if the purchaser goes through with the transaction, the purchaser could maintain a private action for the costs of cleanup against the seller. In this situation, the seller, although liable, would have no control of cleanup activities. Further, operations as conducted by the purchaser after closing could aggravate existing contamination of the site, further increasing cleanup costs. Thus, to avoid liability, the seller may have the burden of establishing that all contamination was actually caused by the subsequent purchaser.

6.3.2 Disclosure of Available Information

The contract of sale should impose a duty upon the seller to provide the buyer any information in the seller's possession regarding potential environmental concerns. This information would include any permits, monitoring or sample reports, all waste manifests, any process compliance reports, consultant's reports, site plans, aerial photographs, information on process design, correspondence with regulatory agencies, inspection reports, notices of violation, complaints from adjacent property owners, etc.

Frequently, the buyer will request this information in the form of a questionnaire/disclosure statement. If this alternative is chosen, the seller's duty to complete the questionnaire should be included as a condition in the contract. The questionnaire should also seek any knowledge the seller may have regarding environmental compliance or contamination. Further, the contract should indicate that the questionnaire will be certified by the seller and will also be incorporated in the closing documents.

The seller should not seek to limit this provision. First, providing all available information up front will avoid the need to renegotiate the transaction if the purchaser learns of the information through independent means. Further, any attempt by the seller to withhold information of which it has knowledge could subject the seller to potential misrepresentation claims. Finally, including "as is" clauses in the contract will not protect the seller from future claims by the buyer.[2] Caveat emptor ("buyer beware" doctrine) is not a defense to private actions under CERCLA.[3]

6.3.3 Scope of the Environmental Site Assessment

The contract must provide the purchaser or his agents the authority to conduct appropriate investigations regarding the property, i.e., the environmental site assessment. This should include the right to inspect the property, talk to present and former employees, inspect records, take samples, conduct surface and subsurface investigations as deemed necessary by the purchaser, etc. The purchaser should also seek authority to contact any regulatory agency regarding the compliance history of the site (although the purchaser already has this right without the contract provision, it is recommended that the seller be put on notice of the purchaser's intent to contact the various agencies).

The environmental site assessment conducted by the buyer may, however, subject the seller to liability. The assessment may uncover previously unknown contamination or past regulatory violations. As indicated above, many environmental statutes have reporting provisions (e.g., releases of hazardous materials in excess of reportable quantities under CERCLA) requiring the owner or operator of a facility to report certain releases to the appropriate regulatory agency. The newly discovered contamination or violations may have to be reported to the appropriate agency. Depending on their magnitude, the regulatory agency may require remediation of the site or seek appropriate penalties. As a result, the seller would have to either expend funds to cover the cleanup or reduce the purchase price to reflect the anticipated costs. In the event the purchaser seeks to terminate the transaction because of the contamination, the seller would have to generate funds from a source other than the purchase price to remediate the site.

If the purchaser wishes to conduct sampling on the property, the contract should allow the seller to retain its own technical consultant to review and approve the sampling plan prior to implementation. The seller should also request copies of all sampling reports and analyses and require confidentiality in the event the sale does not close (subject, of course, to the reporting requirements of any applicable statutes). The seller should also seek indemnification for any damages incurred as a result of the purchaser's consultant's activities.

The seller may want to limit the extent of employee contacts. If the terms of the transfer have not yet been finalized, the seller may not have disclosed the possibility of a sale to his labor force. The purchaser's inquiries, however, may disclose this information prematurely. Clearly, this consideration must be considered on a case-by-case basis.

The seller should also seek to control all contacts with the regulatory agencies. If contamination in excess of reportable quantities is encountered, the contract should provide that this data be reported by the seller. The buyer's inquiries may also raise suspicions among the agencies, subjecting the seller's operation to unnecessary regulatory scrutiny. While this concern is generally unfounded for inquiries at the federal or state level, local inquiries may result in additional inspections of the property.

In the event the investigation concludes that there is little likelihood of contamination, or that the seller has successfully completed cleanup of known contamination on the property, the seller may also request a release from both the buyer and any lenders involved in the transaction. Because any deficiency in the cleanup would take time to manifest itself, however, the buyer will typically be reluctant to give a release to the seller.

6.3.4 Warranties, Representations, and Indemnifications

The buyer should seek a tight set of warranties and representations from the seller regarding past and present activities on the site. The seller should represent the completeness and accuracy of all information requested above, the compliance history of the operation, any past or current violations, any known contamination on the site, off-site waste disposal, etc. The warranties and representations should be worded to include both actual and constructive knowledge of the seller, and also indicate that the seller made significant inquiries before making the representations. Indemnification for omissions or misrepresentations should also be specifically provided. Finally, because potential environmental problems will not become immediately apparent, the warranties and representations must survive closing.

Depending on the type of property involved in the transaction, the purchaser should also seek complete indemnification for any environmental liability imposed on the purchaser that results from past activities, including off-site liabilities. Because of the difficulty in proving causation, special care should be given in drafting these provisions to cover future liabilities. As an example, assume the purchaser incurs a civil penalty for a violation of a discharge permit that occurs after closing. The buyer should seek indemnifications that would cover the violation if it were caused by the seller's faulty design of the treatment system prior to acquisition. Finally, as with any indemnification protection, the indemnification is only as good as the seller's ability to satisfy the indemnification obligation. Because of the potential magnitude of liability, the buyer may also consider seeking to have the indemnifications secured with appropriate escrow accounts funded by a portion of the purchase price.

The seller, however, will seek to limit these warranties, representations, and indemnifications to the extent possible. First, all terms included within these provisions should be fully defined. The seller should also seek to limit the time during which the warranties and representations that survive closing could be enforced against the seller. The seller will also seek to limit its indemnification obligation to those costs arising out of its ownership or operation of the property. Examples of indemnification language are included in Appendix D.

The seller should also negotiate the indemnification to provide a limit to possible exposure. The seller may also seek to include a deductible in the indemnification or language providing that any cleanup costs would be apportioned between the parties. Finally, the seller should also seek indemnification from the buyer in the event the buyer's future activities would subject the seller to future administrative or legal costs.

6.3.5 Contract Termination Clause

The most important contract provision is the "kick-out clause" that allows the buyer to cancel the transaction because of potential environmental concerns revealed during the site assessment. Generally, these provisions will provide an investigation period during which the buyer may conduct the assessment. The length of this period is subject to negotiation and depends on the size and complexity of the property being acquired. The purchaser should also seek provisions allowing for the extension of this period in the event certain types of potential problems are encountered.

The seller should seek to limit the buyer's ability to terminate the contract to specific situations or a minimum magnitude of damages. The contract should also provide the seller the opportunity, at his option, to cure any minor environmental hazards revealed during the assessment prior to the purchaser's termination of the transaction. This will prevent the buyer from having an open-door contract that he could terminate at will.

The seller should also seek to obtain the ability to terminate the contract in the event contamination is found during the assessment. This would allow the seller to control the cleanup in the event remediation is required. Otherwise, the seller could be subject to double liability. For example, assume the seller reduces the purchase price to cover the anticipated cost to clean up contamination found as part of the site assessment. After closing, however, the seller loses all control over the property. If the buyer does not adequately clean up the site, the seller remains liable for the cleanup of the contamination that existed at the time of the transfer. Thus, the seller could still incur cleanup costs even though he accepted a reduced price for the property.

The provision for contract termination is considered the most important for two reasons. First, it gives the parties the ability to terminate the transaction if major, unanticipated liabilities are encountered. Secondly, and more importantly, by giving one or both parties the limited ability to terminate the transaction, it also gives them the ability to restructure or renegotiate in the event additional information is generated during the investigation phase. The relative strengths of the parties' ability to terminate the contract will govern the parties' incentive or bargaining position to restructure the transaction if required in the future.

6.4 STRUCTURING THE TRANSACTION

6.4.1 Creating a Separate Corporate Identity To Take Title

Although it is virtually impossible to eliminate all risk, the purchaser can structure the transaction to at least reduce that risk. Perhaps the most common method utilized by purchasers to reduce risk is to purchase the property through a separate entity. While the assets of the newly formed entity would remain at risk, this structure would tend to protect other assets held by the purchaser.

If this vehicle is chosen, the purchaser must maintain the separate corporate identity of the new entity. In addition to having a legitimate business purpose, the new entity must maintain separate corporate control (i.e., different management, board of directors, etc.) and be adequately capitalized to maintain a separate corporate identity. Further, cases like Ventron, NEPACCO, and Conservation Chemical (see Chapter 2), would indicate that the parent company's involvement in the day-to-day activities of the subsidiary could subject the parent corporation to potential liability.[4] Where, however, the two entities adhere closely to basic corporate formalities by keeping their books, records, meetings, and daily operations strictly separate, the parent may avoid liability.[5]

The EPA has also issued a guidance memorandum addressing the liability of successor corporations under CERCLA.[6] This guidance indicates that the EPA will seek to impose liability on a parent corporation under a public interest theory. The EPA takes the position that the "corporate entity may be disregarded in the interests of public convenience, fairness and equity," and that the federal courts will "look closely at the purpose of the federal statute to determine whether that statute places importance on the corporate form." As a result, the EPA concludes that the courts may use the language of CERCLA either as a rationale for piercing the corporate veil or as an independent statutory basis for imposing liability. The U.S. District Court of Michigan, however, has recently held that corporate successor liability does not extend to CERCLA liability.[7]

6.4.2 Asset Purchase Vs Stock Purchase

If the transaction involves the acquisition of an existing corporation, the purchaser has several options regarding the transfer. A successor corporation's liability is dependent on the structure of the corporate acquisition.[8] The most common methods of transferring a corporate interest include:

1. sale of outstanding stock;
2. merger or consolidation with another corporation; or
3. sale of all assets.

Generally, where the corporation is acquired through the sale of outstanding stock or a statutory consolidation or merger, the successor corporation retains the liabilities of the predecessor corporation.[9] Where only the assets of the corporation are acquired, however, the successor is generally not liable for the debts or liabilities of the predecessor corporation.[10] As a result, purchasing only the assets of a corporation may allow the acquiring entity to avoid the selling corporation's past environmental liability.

The courts have carved out four general exceptions where the corporation acquiring the assets of another corporation may also be responsible for the debts and liabilities of the predecessor. These exceptions include:

1.   the purchaser expressly or impliedly agrees to assume such obligations;
2.   the transaction amounts to a "de facto" consolidation or merger;
3.   the purchasing corporation is merely a continuation of the predecessor; or
4.   the transaction is entered into fraudulently to escape liability.[11]

Consummating the transaction via an asset purchase instead of a stock purchase may be beneficial in some circumstances to avoid such liabilities as past permit violations and penalties, off-site liability under CERCLA, past common law claims, or potential toxic tort claims. This structure, however, will not avoid postacquisition liability for on-site remediation costs imposed by CERCLA or RCRA. Further, this type of transaction may also be overly cumbersome in that any permits held by the predecessor must be transferred to the successor.

If any of the permits held by the predecessor corporation are not transferable, the successor corporation would have to reapply to the appropriate regulatory agency seeking issuance of a new permit authorizing the same activity. This application may subject the facility to a complete review. Closing could be delayed if the permits are not issued in a timely manner. Further, reapplication may cause the facility to lose certain "grandfathered" rights included in the previous permits, e.g., "preexisting source status." As a result, the successor corporation may be subject to more stringent regulatory controls.

Because of these transfer problems, it is usually easier to use a stock transfer, with the seller providing indemnification for suspected potential liability. Where potential past liabilities may be high or are impossible to accurately assess, the asset purchase alternative may be advisable.

6.4.3 Lease With Option to Purchase

If significant concerns exist regarding the potential liabilities associated with the property, the purchaser may also consider leasing the property with an option to purchase at a later date. This would allow the purchaser additional time to evaluate both the property and the operations prior to acquisition. If this alternative is chosen, the lease should contain provisions indemnifying the lessee for liability resulting from past activities of the lessor (it is also likely that the lessor would require indemnification for liabilities resulting from future activities of the lessee). Sample lease indemnification language is included in Appendix D.

Recent case law has indicated, however, that a lessee can be held liable as an owner or operator of the facility.[12] As a result, the lessee could become liable for all on-site cleanup costs. Guidance provided above would also indicate that the EPA will continue to include lessees in the scope of responsible parties. Therefore, if this alternative is chosen, the lease must be carefully drafted to limit the lessee's activities and also specifically limit the areas of the site under the lessee's control. The lease should provide that the lessor will indemnify the lessee for any liability incurred as a result of contamination caused by past activities or activities conducted on other portions of the site not controlled by the lessee. Similarly, the lease should also provide that the lessee will indemnify the lessor for any environmental contamination incurred as a result of the lessee's activities. As noted in previous chapters, CERCLA will impose liability on the owner who leases to a disposing party.

6.5 ALTERNATIVES WHEN POTENTIAL ENVIRONMENTAL LIABILITY IS ENCOUNTERED

When potential environmental liability is encountered, the parties must first determine the appropriate procedures pursuant to the contract of sale. In order to evaluate the extent of the risk, the estimated cost to remediate the facility must also be determined. If the type of liability is such that the potential maximum exposure can be readily determined, and this amount is relatively small when compared to the total purchase price, it is likely that the parties can successfully renegotiate the transaction. The purchaser must be aware, however, that because he is now purchasing the property with knowledge of the contamination, he may no longer avail himself of the innocent purchaser defense or the *de minimis* settlement provisions.

Some of the options available to the parties in this situation include:

1. terminating the transaction;
2. delaying closing until remediation completed;
3. closing transaction with a reduced purchase price;
4. closing transaction, buyer maintains private action against seller for contribution or indemnification; and
5. closing transaction, fund escrow account to pay for remediation.

The applicability of one or more of these alternatives will clearly depend on the site-specific characteristics of the property involved in the transaction. The ability of you or your client to take advantage of these alternatives, however, will depend on the foresight exercised during the negotiation of the contract of sale.

6.5.1 Terminate the Transaction

As discussed above, the contract should provide certain guidelines whereby either party can terminate the contract provided certain threshold conditions are met. The buyer should consider exercising his termination rights when the potential liability is high compared to the uncontaminated value of the property or when the potential costs are difficult to accurately predict. The seller should terminate when potential liabilities are such that improper handling could greatly magnify the problem. After closing, the seller loses control over the site. Thus, it may be more advantageous for the seller to cancel the present transaction, correct the problem, and then begin renegotiation with the same or new prospective purchaser.

6.5.2 Delay Closing Until Remediation Completed

If the environmental hazards encountered during the assessment stage are minor and easily quantifiable, the parties may want to delay closing to allow appropriate remediation of the site by the seller. This alternative is frequently used when the contract provides the seller the right to remediate the hazard prior to contract termination. If the seller chooses to clean up the site, the scope of the remediation plan must be fully negotiated prior to cleanup. The buyer will generally require that the remediation be coordinated with applicable regulatory agencies, and also may seek confirmation from those agencies that remediation activities conducted prior to closing have adequately resolved the problem. The seller, on the other hand, will typically require that he obtain a release from the purchaser, thereby precluding any additional actions by the purchaser against the seller. Each party's requirements with respect to regulatory review and releases should be addressed and agreed to prior to the expenditure of funds towards remediation.

6.5.3 Close Transaction With Reduced Purchase Price

This alternative is similar to the one above and is generally used where potential liabilities are small and easily defined. Usually the reduction in the purchase price is equal to the estimated cost of remediation plus a factor of safety, which can range from 10% to 100% or higher, depending on the type of liability. The difference between this and the previous alternative, however, is that this alternative shifts the risk of a complete cleanup from the seller to the buyer. Although the seller would remain liable to the government under statute, the regulatory agencies would most likely look first to the present landowner. Because the subsequent purchaser acquired the property with knowledge and benefited from a reduced purchase price, it is unlikely that liability could be avoided. While the purchaser might have the right to recover damages from the seller, the seller may not have sufficient assets or may have obtained a release from the purchaser in return for the reduction in purchase price. Therefore, any purchaser utilizing this alternative must be fully aware of the potential risks and be confident that the price abatement will adequately cover remediation costs.

6.5.4 Close Transaction With Buyer
Maintaining Private Action Against Seller

If the parties do not choose to terminate the contract and cannot agree on appropriate price reductions, the purchaser can proceed to closing and remediate the site after closing. The purchaser could then maintain a private action against the seller for the costs of the remediation. This alternative, however, is extremely risky from the purchaser's prospective. First, it is seldom wise to buy into litigation. Second, the seller would advance equitable arguments that the purchase price had already been reduced to reflect the environmental hazards. Because the purchaser had prior knowledge of the contamination, this argument would most likely carry weight.[13] Finally, if the seller was appropriately counseled prior to closing, the seller would have sought a release prior to closing.

6.5.5 Close Transaction, Fund Escrow
Account to Pay For Remediation

The negotiation of an escrow agreement to fund future remediation activities is perhaps the best alternative for addressing newly encountered environmental hazards. As with the other alternatives, this alternative should only be used when the required remediation is small when compared to the purchase price or can be accurately identified. Generally, this alternative involves the negotiation of an agreement that takes a portion of the proceeds of the purchase price and places those funds in escrow to cover the cost of certain remediation activities described in the escrow agreement.

The amount of the escrow should be enough to cover the estimated cost of the activities, and should also include an adequate contingency (10% to 100% of the estimated escrow amount). The agreement should clearly define what activities will be conducted, who will perform the activities, when funds will be disbursed, what performance standards will be met, the involvement of regulatory agencies, who controls contact with the agencies, etc. The agreement can also provide for cost sharing between the parties or provide a deductible amount that must first be reached prior to the expenditure of escrow funds.

The escrow agreement must provide a termination date when remaining funds, if any, will be returned to the seller. Obviously, the term of the agreement is subject to negotiation and depends on the scope of activities to be conducted. In return for agreeing to the establishment of the fund, however, the seller will typically seek a complete release from the purchaser. As always, this too is subject to negotiation.

6.6 CONCLUSION

This chapter outlines the various considerations of the purchaser and seller throughout the course of the transaction. Clearly, all property acquisitions must be preceded by an environmental site assessment to allow the purchaser to qualify for applicable defenses, as well as adequately apprise the parties of the regulatory status of the property. The scope of the assessment is determined by both past and present uses of the property and the operation's compliance history. If the site assessment determines that there is little likelihood of potential liability, the purchaser may qualify for the innocent purchaser defense or a *de minimis* landowner settlement in the event on-site contamination is encountered in the future. The contract should also provide a tight set of warranties and representations, as well as indemnifications, in the event the purchaser incurs future liability for past activities. The contract should also provide appropriate termination provisions should unexpected contamination be encountered.

In the event the site assessment reveals potential liability, the parties should not be too quick to terminate the transaction. If the extent of the liability is small or easily defined, alternatives exist to allow the consummation of the transaction. The establishment of an escrow agreement is usually the safest alternative for reducing risk and adequately remediating the property. The following chapter will provide illustrative examples on how these alternatives could be implemented.

REFERENCES

1. *New York v. Shore Realty Corp.*, 759 F.2d 1032 (2d Cir. 1985); *United States v. Maryland Bank & Trust Company*, 632 F.Supp. 573 (D.Md. 1986).
2. *Mardan Corp. v. C.G.C. Music Ltd.*, 804 F.2d 1454 (9th Cir. 1986); *Chemical Waste Management v. Armstrong World Industries*, 669 F. Supp. 1285 (E.D.Pa. 1987); *International Clinical Laboratories, Inc. v. Stevens*, 710 F.Supp 466 (E.D.N.Y. 1989).
3. *Smith Land & Improvement Company v. Celotex Corp.*, 851 F.2d 86 (3rd Cir. 1988).
4. *State Dept. of Environ. Protect. v. Ventron*, 468 A.2d 150 (N.J. 1983); *United States v. Northeastern Pharmaceutical & Chemical Co., Inc.*, 810 F.2d 726 (8th Cir. 1986); *United States v. Conservation Chemicals Company*, 628 F. Supp. 391 (W.D.Mo. 1986); *United States v. Kayser-Roth Corp.*, 724 F.Supp. 15 (D.R.I. 1989).
5. *Joslyn Corp. v. T. L. James & Co.*, No. 88-4901 (5th Cir. Jan. 29, 1990).
6. U.S. Environmental Protection Agency Guidance Memorandum, June 13, 1984.

7. *Anspec Co. v. Johnson Controls Inc.,* No.89-CV-71165-DT (Sept. 25, 1989).

8. *New Jersey Transportation Dept. v. P.S.C. Resources, Inc.,* 175 N.J. Super. 447, 419 A.2d 1151 (1980).

9. Fletcher, W. "Cyclopedia of the Law of Private Corporations," Vol. 15, Sec. 7121 (rev. perm. ed. 1983), p. 185.

10. *Polius v. Clark Equipment Co.,* 802 F.2d 75,77 (3d Cir. 1986).

11. "Torts — Products Liability — Successor Corporation Strictly Liable for Defective Products Manufactured By the Predecessor Corporation," Villanova Law Review, Vol. 27 (1980), p. 411.

12. *United States v. Argent Corp.,* 14 E.L.R. 20616 (D.N.M. 1984); see also *United States v. South Carolina Recycling, Inc.,* 14 E.L.R. 20895 (D.S.C. 1984).

13. *Smith Land & Improvement Corp. v. Celotex Corp.,* 851 F.2d 86 (3rd Cir. 1988).

CHAPTER 7

Hypothetical Case Studies

CHAPTER CONTENTS

Hypothetical Case Studies

7.1 INTRODUCTION

In the preceding chapters, the authors have endeavored to provide the technical and legal principles necessary to understand basic environmental liability issues and how to minimize this liability. This chapter will take these principles and apply them to five hypothetical case studies. Each case study provides a different situation involving real estate and potential environmental liability.

The following format is used to present each case study:

1. Description of case
2. Environmental site assessment needs
3. Potential results of the assessment
4. Effects on the "deal"

The first section of each case study provides a description of the case, including who the interested parties are and why they need to be concerned with potential environmental liabilities. The second section outlines the likely scope of the environmental site assessment for each case study. The third section offers examples of potential results of the site assessment. The last section examines the effects of the assessment results on the transaction and demonstrates how the transaction can be adjusted to meet the parties' needs.

These hypothetical case studies should provide the reader with a good idea of when environmental site assessments are needed, the scope of the assessments, and how the assessment results could affect the particular transaction. These case studies represent real-life situations where environmental liability is a factor; however, no case is based on a particular site.

7.2 CASE STUDIES

7.2.1 A Manufacturing Company Applies for a Loan to Expand Facilities

Description of Case
ABC company manufactures electronic instruments at their Greenburgh

plant. The company wants to expand the plant to increase its capacity. The company applies for a loan from the First Bank. First Bank's policy requires that the loan be secured by the present and future facilities. Because the First Bank could potentially foreclose on the property should ABC default on its loan, the First Bank requires the company to conduct an environmental site assessment of the property and current plant to ensure the integrity of the security. Further, the ability of ABC to satisfy its loan obligation depends on the continuation of current operations. Thus, the assessment will also provide insights as to potential future compliance problems that may be encountered.

Environmental Site Assessment Needs

The environmental site assessment for this case study should consist of at least the following activities:

1. title search for past owners;
2. inspection of the property for signs of contamination;
3. comprehensive audit of facility operations for environmental violations and for past hazardous material and waste handling procedures; and
4. contacting applicable environmental regulatory agencies to determine if there have been any reports of contamination or violations at the facility or neighboring properties.

Potential Results of the Assessment

The site assessment will generally identify any apparent or known environmental problems at the facility. For this hypothetical case, we will assume that no contamination of the property was found, but several environmental violations were noted during the audit of the plant and through contacts with environmental agencies. Although these violations did not result in releases to the environment requiring further investigation or cleanup, the violations could result in both civil and/or criminal penalties being levied against the owner or operator of the facility.

Effects on the "Deal"

The First Bank's review of the site assessment results indicates that the Bank is not likely to assume any significant environmental liability resulting from past activities on the site. The bank's primary concern would focus on the impact that potential penalties may have on its borrower's ability to satisfy its debt obligation. First Bank decides to approve the loan conditioned upon correction of the violations and receipt of a letter from the applicable environmental agencies certifying that the problems have been corrected. The bank may also require that an escrow account be created that would apply to any penalties. This escrow would be funded at closing out of either the purchase price or the proceeds of the loan. In addition, the bank may seek to limit future activities on the site by including covenants in the loan documents preventing the storage, treatment, handling, or disposal of hazardous materials on the property.

7.2.2 A Corporation Seeks to Acquire a Manufacturing Plant

Description of Case

XYZ corporation is interested in purchasing the Browntown plant from Acme Corporation. The Browntown plant produced rolled steel for about 30 years up until one year ago when the plant was shut down. The XYZ corporation desires to reopen the plant to produce rolled steel and other steel-related products. XYZ takes the position, however, that the sale price, although market value, does not adequately reflect potential remediation costs associated with the site. Acme corporation revealed to XYZ that the plant operations had included dumping of pickle liquors and other wastes into an on-site lagoon. This practice continued for a period of 22 years until 1983, at which time the state hazardous waste agency required the company to close the lagoon pursuant to RCRA closure requirements. The lagoon was closed and postclosure groundwater monitoring has shown relatively insignificant levels of pollutants. No other environmental problems were disclosed by the seller.

Environmental Site Assessment Needs

The assessment for this case study should review all past site activities and waste practices, with special emphasis on investigating the lagoon that was closed pursuant to RCRA closure requirements. The related items to investigate and evaluate include the method used to close the facility, the adequacy of the method to prevent hazardous material releases, and what the costs of postclosure groundwater monitoring are. Beyond the known instance of environmental contamination, there may be others that have not been revealed or are not known by Acme Corporation. A title search should be conducted to identify all prior owners and operations.

An investigation of the plant and surrounding property will be conducted to look for other signs of contamination. Because the plant is shut down, an audit of the plant's operations cannot be performed. However, the plant's operating records, particularly with regard to waste treatment, handling, and disposal, should be available and reviewed.

All applicable environmental agencies will be contacted to determine what environmental violations and releases have occurred at the plant. In particular, the agency (and agency staff if still employed by the agency) that was involved with the closure of the pond should be contacted for information on the closure and postclosure of the pond.

Because of the known problem of the closed pond and the nature of operations that existed at the plant, the site assessment must include subsurface investigations in addition to resampling the groundwater monitoring wells currently existing around the pond to ensure that no other contamination exists.

These investigations would include soil borings and additional groundwater sampling. If possible, sampling on adjacent properties should also be done to check for migration of pollutants off-site.

The site assessment should also look at off-site methods for disposal of hazardous waste generated by the Browntown plant during its operations. This is important for determining if any of the disposal sites used by the plant have or could become listed as waste sites that may require cleanup, thus potentially subjecting XYZ corporation to cleanup costs under CERCLA or applicable state laws.

Potential Results of the Assessment

The assessment determined that there was further contamination on-site, although not as extensive as that of the pond. The assessment further found that one of the disposal sites formerly utilized by Browntown is being investigated by the EPA as a potential Superfund site.

Effects on the Deal

Upon reviewing the results of the assessment, XYZ corporation has essentially two options: (1) cancel the transaction or (2) renegotiate the price and/or the conditions of the sale. The price could be adjusted to reflect potential cleanup costs. Another alternative would be for Browntown to clean up the site prior to transfer. With regard to potential liability for cleanup of the off-site waste disposal site, Acme should be required to indemnify XYZ against any liability resulting from wastes disposed of at the site. Because of the potential joint and several liability for the off-site concerns, XYZ should be very cautious before buying into this potential liability.

7.2.3 A Corporation Seeks to Acquire Another Corporation

Description of Case

Shark Corporation is interested in acquiring a majority of stock of Enco Corporation. Enco is a diverse corporation that owns a number of manufacturing plants, warehouses, and commercial properties. The Shark Corporation will likely continue to operate these properties as Enco did, with the exception of selling certain manufacturing plants to reduce debt that will be incurred in buying Enco.

As in the previous case study, Shark needs to determine if environmental problems exist at any of Enco's properties that could result in expensive cleanup costs, fines, or lawsuits and delay sale of assets. Enco, however, does not want to be bought by Shark and consequently will not provide any information to Shark on the status of the properties.

Environmental Site Assessment Needs

As a result of the adverse relationship between the buyer and seller in this case study, the environmental site assessments of Enco's properties will be difficult and limited. It is likely that the assessment team conducting the assessment will not be allowed access to the properties to make on-site investigations. Consequently, extra efforts will need to be made to determine environmental contamination violations and liability through other means including the following:

1. title search to identify former owners or operators;
2. contacting applicable environmental agencies to determine any past environmental violations or releases (review of agencies' files on Enco properties can reveal a wealth of information);
3. review of manifests maintained by agencies that identify off-site shipments of hazardous wastes;
4. review of aerial photographs;
5. contacting fire and health departments to provide further information on potential violations; and
6. interviews with former employees, neighbors, or vendors of Enco.

Though these efforts cannot fully substitute for on-site investigations and access to company records, they may uncover many environmental problems that would otherwise be unknown to the prospective buyer.

Potential Results of the Assessment

The investigations conducted under the limited assessment described above determined that indeed there were several cases of potentially expensive environmental liabilities. These included ongoing air and water pollution violations at one plant, which would require investment of capital for control equipment; contamination at one site reported by a former employee, the extent of which is unknown; and a significant quantity of hazardous materials reportedly stored at one of Enco's warehouses, which if released to the environment through fire, explosion, spill, or other means could subject the company to expensive cleanup costs, fines, and lawsuits.

Effects on the "Deal"

The environmental site assessment team, in conjunction with financial analysts, put together best, worst, and most likely case estimates for potential environmental liability costs of buying Enco Corporation. Although the worst case estimate would make the acquisition unprofitable, the most likely and best case estimates could be covered through sale of acquired assets and mitigation of problems by Shark's consultants and attorneys. Consequently, it was decided that Shark corporation would proceed with acquisition.

7.2.4 A Commercial Property Owner has Tenants that Handle Hazardous Materials

Description of Case

A commercial property is owned by an individual. The property houses multiple tenants including a body shop, pesticide applicator, swimming pool supply outlet, and an auto parts machine and plating shop. These tenants all store some form of hazardous materials, including paints, solvents, pesticides, chlorine, degreasers, acid, and plating baths. The property owner is concerned that one of the tenants may contaminate his property or release hazardous materials to the environment and cause the owner to be liable for related cleanup costs and fines.

Environmental Site Assessment Needs

The property owner is most concerned with the operations of his tenants that store hazardous materials. The assessment will consist of first inspecting all the property owner's tenants to determine if any hazardous materials are present. The tenants that do store hazardous materials will then be audited to determine how the hazardous materials are handled, if the materials are used in any operations, signs of contamination, and the potential for release of the hazardous materials. The assessment should also involve contacting applicable environmental agencies to determine if any of the tenants have had environmental violations.

Potential Results of the Assessment

The assessment determined that the body shop and pool supply outlet pose minimal liability due to their methods for using and storing hazardous materials and the kinds and form of hazardous materials present. However, the pesticide applicator and auto parts machine and plating shop are both poorly operated and have been responsible for releases of hazardous materials to the environment. The pesticide applicator occasionally rinses out trucks with the rinse water draining to a stormwater culvert. The machine and plating shop has been cited several times by the local sewage treatment plant authority for violation of the metal finishing categorical pretreatment standards for new sources and by the local hazardous waste authority for improper storage of hazardous wastes.

Effects on the "Deal"

The transaction in this case is the continued leasing of the premises to the various tenants. The property owner should take immediate steps to force the pesticide applicator to stop all practices resulting in the discharge of wastes to the stormwater culvert and the ground around the property.

In the case of the auto parts machining and plating shop, the property owner should consider terminating the lease if such provisions are provided by the lease agreement. If not, the owner should seek to force the tenant to come into compliance with applicable regulations within a reasonable time.

This case demonstrates the importance of including "environmental compliance" language in the lease, with appropriate termination language for noncompliance. Furthermore, the property owner may also want to consider restricting leases to tenants who do not handle hazardous materials.

7.2.5 A Developer Seeks to Acquire a Large Farm for Residential Development

Description of Case

In this example, a residential development company seeks to acquire a large undeveloped parcel of property. The company intends to subdivide the property to provide individual single family residential units. There are currently no active operations on the property. The property contains one residential structure occupied by the current owner, as well as numerous barns and outbuildings. Prior to retiring, the owner of the property owned and operated a small construction and landscaping company. Some of the buildings on the property were used to provide storage areas for materials and equipment used during operations. The owner has also indicated that one of the buildings was used for a shop to service the equipment, and also that several underground storage tanks exist in this area that were used to store fuel for the equipment.

Environmental Site Assessment Needs

In addition to the document searches, agency contacts, site inspection, and owner/operator interview activities conducted as part of all Phase I site assessments, the site assessment in this case should also investigate the following issues:

1. specific buildings and areas of the property involved in prior operations;
2. types of equipment stored on the site;
3. types and quantities of materials handled;
4. description of activities and waste practices conducted in the former shop, including equipment maintenance records;
5. size, age, and type of underground storage tanks, including any records available regarding the tanks; and
6. type and quantity of materials stored in the tanks.

Areas previously used as equipment storage and shop areas have frequently been contaminated with waste motor and hydraulic oils used in the equipment. Depending on the scope of maintenance activities conducted in the shop, solvents and degreasers may also have been used in the repair of the equipment. Many times these waste materials have been disposed of or stored on the site. As a result, the assessment must look for stained soils or old storage drums in these areas. If any of these indicators are found, the area should be sampled and analyzed for suspected contaminants.

If the shop area contained floor drains or wash basins, these materials may have been discharged to the sewer system. If the sewer system consists of an on-site septic system, any materials discharged to the basin or floor drains would be discharged directly to the surrounding soils. If these activities are suspected, the soils in the on-site drainfield should also be sampled and analyzed.

The assessment must also address any potential contamination that may have resulted from the underground storage tanks. This evaluation could include either review of tank integrity test results or subsurface sample analyses collected from borings surrounding the tanks. Because the tanks are no longer used or needed for future operations, it would be in the buyer's best interest to require that the tanks be removed and the excavation sampled prior to closing. Removal of the tanks would not only uncover any existing contamination, but would also save the buyer the expense of removing and disposing of the tanks in the future.

Potential Results of the Assessment

Obviously, if all of the sampling activities described above are conducted and no elevated levels of contamination are encountered, the transaction should be completed. Thus, for purposes of this example, it will be assumed that interviews with the owner indicated the following:

1. waste oils were shipped back to supplier for recycling;
2. small quantities of oils were spilled on unpaved areas during routine mainte-nance of equipment;
3. there is no history of solvents being used on the property; and
4. the tanks are 15-year-old steel tanks and have never been tested.

Site inspections have revealed localized soil staining in the maintenance areas described by the owner. Soil borings have limited the area of contamina-tion to about 200 square feet and shown contamination to a depth of only one foot, with sample analyses indicating total petroleum hydrocarbon (TPH) levels of 80 ppm. The one soil boring conducted adjacent to the tanks, however, has shown TPH levels of over 200 ppm at a depth of eight feet, the depth of the seasonably high groundwater in the area.

Effects on the "Deal"

The problems created by the surface soil contamination are relatively minor and should not have a significant impact on the transaction. The limits of the contamination are well defined and do not involve large quantities of soils. It is likely that the total cost of remediation of this area could be accurately estimated. Funds to cover this expense, plus a reasonable contingency, could then be placed in escrow at closing to ensure the future cleanup and disposal of the soils.

The tanks create a more complex problem. Because of the levels of contamination encountered and the level of groundwater in the area, it is likely that significant quantities of soils have been contaminated. It is also likely that groundwater in the area has also been contaminated and needs remediation. Because of the uncertainty associated with the tanks, the buyer should delay closing until the tanks have been removed and all contaminated soils have been treated or removed and disposed of to the satisfaction of the applicable regulatory agency. In the event the seller is unwilling or does not have adequate resources to complete this cleanup, the buyer could proceed to closing and once again escrow funds to cover the remediation costs from the purchase price. Because of the open questions as to the extent of contamination, the buyer is assuming significant risk by choosing the latter option. This risk could be mitigated, however, by providing a significant contingency allowance in the escrow account.

7.3 CONCLUSION

The preceding case studies illustrate the basic principles and concepts outlined in this book. As discussed, recent environmental trends have made buyers and lenders potentially responsible for environmental liabilities associated with newly acquired property. By conducting appropriate activities, buyers and lenders can reduce their potential exposure when property is acquired or financed. These activities include the following:

1.   Conducting an environmental site assessment prior to acquisition or financing; and
2.   Properly structuring the transaction to address environmental concerns.

Through the case studies in this chapter (and the examples in Chapter 5), the authors have endeavored to identify common sources of environmental liabilities. In addition, the case studies have shown how environmental liabilities can affect buyers, sellers, and financiers of property. These concepts are important to the layperson who is trying to understand the results of the site assessment and apply these results to the transaction.

As a final note, this book has covered a wide variety of environmental issues relating to property transfer and financing. As with any handbook covering so many topics, specific details of each topic may not be presented. The reader is encouraged to review additional texts on environmental issues of interest. In addition, the reader should seek professional legal and technical assistance where necessary and appropriate.

GLOSSARY

Aquifer:	A geologic formation, group of formations, or part of a formation capable of yielding a significant amount of groundwater to wells or springs.
ARARs:	ARARs is an acronym for Applicable or Relevant and Appropriate Requirements and refers to those standards and requirements promulgated under various environmental laws that are used for cleanup of hazardous waste sites under CERCLA.
Carcinogen:	Any material known to cause or suspected of causing cancer in a living organism.
CERCLA:	The Comprehensive Environmental Response, Compensation, and Liability Act passed in 1980 and commonly known as the "Superfund." CERCLA gives the federal government the power to respond to releases, or threatened releases, of any hazardous substances into the environment as well as to release of a pollutant or contaminant that may present an imminent and substantial danger to public health or welfare. CERCLA established a Hazardous Response Superfund (formerly the Hazardous Substance Response Trust Fund) available to finance responses taken by the federal government.
CERCLIS:	CERCLIS stands for CERCLA Information System, which contains a list of actual and suspected hazardous waste sites grouped by post office zip code.
Chain of custody:	Evidence of analytical data is related to samples taken at particular locations and times. In offering real evidence, the offeror accounts for the custody of evidence from the time it is gathered until the time that it is offered in evidence. If this custody "chain" is broken, the admissibility of evidence can be challenged.

Clean Water Act:	An act passed by Congress to protect the physical, chemical, and biological integrity of the nation's waters. The Federal Water Pollution Control Act was originally passed in 1972. It was later amended in 1976 by the Clean Water Act and in 1987 by the Water Quality Act.
Cleanup:	The elimination, reduction, or containment of pollutants associated with a site in accordance with the National Contingency Plan
Code of Federal Regulations:	U.S. Government Printing Office publication containing all federal regulations. Also known as CFR.
Community right-to-know:	Statutory authority provided by SARA that establishes a state and local emergency planning structure, emergency notification, and reporting requirements for facilities.
Conditional sales contract:	A contract between buyer and seller, wherein the seller reserves title to the property until certain buyer conditions are satisfied.
Confined aquifer:	An aquifer bounded above and below by beds that are impermeable or of distinctly lower permeability than that of the aquifer itself, i.e., an aquifer containing confined groundwater.
Container:	Any portable device in which a material is stored, transported, treated, disposed of, or otherwise handled.
Contingency plan:	A document setting out an organized, planned, and coordinated course of action to be followed in case of a fire, explosion, or release of hazardous waste or hazardous waste constituents that could threaten human health or the environment.
Deed:	A legal document that transfers a property, identifies property owner and partial date of ownership, and describes the property owned.

Deed of trust: A deed containing a statement by the person named as owner of land that he holds title in trust for the use of another person.

Designated facility: A hazardous waste treatment, storage, or disposal facility that has received an EPA permit in accordance with the requirements of 40 CFR Parts 122 and 124 (or a permit from a state authorized in accordance with Part 123), or a facility with interim status.

Dike: An embankment or ridge of either natural or man-made materials used to prevent the movement of liquids, sludges, solids, or other materials.

Direct discharge: The accidental or intentional spilling, leaking, pumping, pouring, emitting, emptying, or dumping of wastewater to surface waters, such as streams, lakes, or oceans.

Disposal: The discharge, deposit, injection, dumping, spilling, leaking, or placing of any solid waste or hazardous waste into or on any land or water.

Disposal facility: A facility or part of a facility at which hazardous waste is intentionally placed into or on any land or water and at which waste will remain after closure.

EPA: The U.S. Environmental Protection Agency.

Facility: All contiguous land and structures, other appurtenances, and improvements on the land used for treating, storing, or disposing of hazardous waste. A facility may consist of several treatment, storage, or disposal operational units (e.g., one or more landfills, surface impoundments, or combinations of them).

Fee simple title: Title to an estate of which the owner is entitled to the entire property, with unconditional power of disposition during his life, and descending to his heirs and legal representatives upon his death.

Generator: Any person or facility whose act or process produces hazardous waste identified or listed in EPA regulations.

Groundwater: Water below the land surface in a zone of saturation.

Hazard Ranking System: The method regulatory agencies use to set priorities for response actions under CERCLA. The Hazard Ranking System (HRS) ranks a site by means of a mathematical rating scheme that combines probability and magnitude. Using the numerical scores, the EPA and the states list sites by priority and allocate resources for site investigation, enforcement, and cleanup. Sites receiving high HRS scores — currently, greater than 28.5 — appear on the National Priorities List.

Hazardous Response Superfund: The Fund, formerly the Hazardous Substance Response Trust Fund, largely financed by an environmental tax on industry that provides operating money for government-financed actions under CERCLA. The Fund is a revolving fund that enables the government to take action and then seek responsible parties when sufficient cleanup funds cannot be found.

Incinerator: An enclosed device using controlled flame combustion, the primary purpose of which is to thermally break down hazardous waste.

Indirect discharge: The discharge of wastewater to the local POTW.

Joint and several liability: The principle whereby the total liability is shared among a group of defendants both collectively and individually.

Land trust: A method of holding real estate. When a land trust is used, the one holding legal title to the land is listed as the trustee on all the legal records. However, by use of a trust agreement, the beneficiary of the trust usually maintains management and control of the real property.

Landfill:	A disposal facility or a part of a facility where hazardous waste is placed in or on land and which is not a land treatment facility, a surface impoundment, or an injection well.
Leachate:	Any liquid, including any suspended components in the liquid, that has percolated through or drained from hazardous waste.
Lease:	A contract by which a landlord rents lands, buildings, and so on to a tenant for a specified time. A lease may provide information on site operations and operators for various periods of time in the site's history.
Lien:	A legal claim on another's property as security for the payment of a just debt. A lien may identify the site's owner and may give an indication of the owner's financial status.
Liner:	A continuous layer of natural or man-made materials, beneath or on the sides of a surface impoundment, landfill, or landfill cell, that restricts the downward or lateral escape of hazardous waste, hazardous waste constituents, or leachate.
Manifest:	The hazardous waste shipping document originated and signed by the generator that contains the information required by EPA regulations.
Material safety data sheet:	A document, usually prepared by the chemical manufacturer, providing a profile of the hazardous materials contained in the material, as well as safety information to be followed in the event of an accident. MSDSs must be maintained for all hazardous materials used or stored in the workplace and be made available to all employees working in these areas.
mg/l:	Milligrams per liter. A unit of measurement indicating pollutant concentration.
Mortgage:	A security interest in land created by a written instrument. Mortgages are usually created to secure payment of a debt.

*National Contingency
Plan:*   A plan (known as NCP) providing for efficient, co-ordinated, and effective response to discharges of oils and releases of hazardous substances.

National Priorities List: The National Priorities List (NPL) establishes priorities for remedial response actions throughout the country through government enforcement action or cleanup (see *Hazard Ranking System).*

Notice letter: The EPA's formal notice to PRPs that CERCLA-related action is to be undertaken at a site for which those PRPs are considered responsible. Notice letters are generally sent at least 60 days prior to scheduled obligation of funds for a remedial investigation/feasibility study at a designated site. The intent is to give PRPs sufficient time to organize and to contact the government.

NPDES permit: A National Pollutant Discharge Elimination System permit is the permit issued to a direct discharger authorizing the regulated discharge of wastewater to surface waters pursuant to the Clean Water Act.

Operator: The person responsible for the overall operation of a facility.

OSHA: The Occupational Safety and Health Administration is the agency responsible for developing and implementing regulations to protect the safety of industrial workers in the workplace.

Owner: The person who owns a facility or part of a facility.

Person: An individual, trust, firm, joint venture, corporation (including a government corporation), partnership, consortium, commercial entity, association, the U.S. Government, state, municipality, commission, political subdivision of a state, or any interstate body.

Point source: Any discernible, confined, and discrete conveyance, including but not limited to any pipe, ditch, channel, tunnel, conduit, well, discrete fissure,

container, rolling stock, concentrated animal feed-
ing operation, vessel, or other floating craft, from
which pollutants are or may be discharged. This
term does not include return flows from irrigated
agriculture.

POTW: Publicly Owned Treatment Works include any
device or system used in the treatment (including
recycling and reclamation) of municipal sewage or
industrial wastes of a liquid nature that is owned by
a state or municipality. This definition includes
sewers, pipes, or other conveyances only if they
convey wastewater to a POTW providing treatment.

ppb: Parts per billion. Unit of measurement indicating
pollutant concentration. For solid and liquid concentrations, a ppb is equivalent to 0.001 mg/l.

ppm: Parts per million. Unit of measurement indicating
pollutant concentration. For solid and liquid concentrations, a ppm is equivalent to 1.0 mg/l.

Proposed NPL sites: Proposed NPL sites are sites which have Hazard
Ranking System scores above 28.5 and are under-
going public comment, but have not yet been added
finally to the NPL.

PRP: Potentially Responsible Parties are those parties
identified by the EPA as potentially liable under
CERCLA for cleanup costs. PRPs may include
generators and other persons who arranged for
disposal or treatment and present or former owners
or operators of certain facilities where hazardous
substances have been located or disposed of, as
well as those who accepted hazardous substances
and transported them to certain facilities.

Quit claim deed: A deed of conveyance, operating by way of release,
that is intended to pass any title, interest, or claim
that the grantor may have on the premises, but not
professing that such title is valid and not containing
any warranty or covenants for title.

RCRA: The Resource Conservation and Recovery Act,

which regulates the generation, storage, transportation, treatment, and disposal of hazardous waste at the federal level. This act is often referred to as the "cradle to grave" statute.

Receiving water: A stream, lake, or other surface or groundwater into which industrial wastewaters are discharged.

Release: The spilling, leaking, pumping, pouring, emitting, emptying, discharging, injecting, escaping, leaching, dumping, or disposing of any hazardous substance into the environment.

Remedial action: A remedy or measure consistent with permanent remedy taken instead of, or in addition to, removal action to prevent or minimize the release or threatened release of hazardous substances so that they do not migrate to cause a substantial danger to present or future public health, welfare, or the environment. Includes a variety of on-site measures (storage, perimeter protection, recycling or reuse, dredging, excavation, etc.), off-site disposition, required monitoring, and the costs of permanent relocation of affected populations when deemed necessary.

Reportable quantity: The minimum quantity of a regulated material, the release of which requires notification to the appropriate regulatory agency.

Representative sample: A sample of a universe or whole (e.g., waste pile, lagoon, groundwater, etc.) that can be expected to exhibit the average properties of the universe or whole.

Responsible party: Party legally liable for response costs pursuant to CERCLA. See *PRP*.

Restrictive covenant: A provision in a deed limiting certain uses of the property.

RI/FS: The Remedial Investigation/Feasibility Study includes an extensive technical investigation conducted by the government or by PRPs to investigate the scope of contamination (RI) and to determine the remedial response, consistent with the NCP, to be implemented at a Superfund site (FS). An RI/FS may include a variety of activities such as monitoring, sampling, and analysis.

Run-off: Any rainwater, leachate, or other liquid that drains over land from any part of a facility.

Run-on: Any rainwater, leachate, or other liquid that drains over land to any part of a facility.

SARA: The Superfund Amendments and Reauthorization Act of 1986 reauthorized CERCLA and increased the "Superfund" to $8.5 billion. SARA emphasizes the importance of developing permanent solutions at hazardous waste sites and imposes requirements for setting cleanup standards. SARA establishes goals and mandatory schedules that the EPA must follow for various phases of remedial response. SARA also sets out procedures for negotiating settlements with potentially responsible parties.

Sludge: Any solid, semisolid, or liquid waste generated from a municipal, commercial, or industrial wastewater treatment plant, water supply treatment plant, or air pollution control facility, exclusive of the treated effluent from a wastewater treatment plant.

Storage: The holding of hazardous waste for a temporary period, at the end of which the hazardous waste is treated, disposed of, or stored elsewhere.

Superfund: See *CERCLA*

Surface impoundment: A facility or part of a facility that is a natural topographic depression, man-made excavation, or diked area formed primarily of earthen materials (although it may be lined with man-made materials), which is designed to hold an accumulation of liquid wastes or wastes containing free liquids, and which is not an injection well. Examples include holding, storage, settling, and aeration pits, ponds, and lagoons.

Tank: A stationary device, designed to contain an accumulation of hazardous waste, that is constructed primarily of nonearthen materials (e.g., wood, concrete, steel, or plastic) that provide structural support.

Technology-based standards:

Discharge limits applicable to a specific industry representing the limits that industry could achieve if it were to use the best treatment technology currently available. These standards are set forth in EPA regulations promulgated pursuant to the Clean Water Act.

Transportation:

Movement of hazardous waste by air, rail, highway, or water.

Transporter:

A person engaged in the off-site transportation of hazardous waste by air, rail, highway, or water.

Treatment:

Any method, technique, or process, including neutralization, designed to change the physical, chemical, or biological character or composition of any hazardous waste so as to neutralize such waste, to recover energy or material resources from the waste, or to render such waste nonhazardous; less hazardous; safer to transport, store, or dispose of; amenable for recovery or storage; or reduced in volume.

Warranty deed:

A deed in which the grantor guarantees to the grantee that the grantor has title to the land free of other possible claims. This document will identify the owner of a site at a particular point in time.

Well:

Any shaft or pit dug or bored into the earth, generally of a cylindrical form, and often walled with bricks or tubing to prevent the earth from caving in.

Statute Citations

Clean Air Act (CAA): 42 U.S.C. 7401 et seq.

Clean Water Act (CWA): 33 U.S.C. 1251 et seq.

Comprehensive Environmental Response, Compensation and Liability Act (CERCLA or Superfund): 42 U.S.C. 9601 et seq.

Occupational Safety and Health Act (OSHA): 29 U.S.C. 651 et seq.

Resource Conservation and Recovery Act (RCRA): 42 U.S.C. 6901 et seq.

Environmental Site Assessment
Checklist Outline

I. General and Historical Information
    A. General Information
    B. Description of Site
    C. Location and Map
    D. Past and Present Environmental Problems
    E. Comments

II. Hazardous Materials Inventory
    A. Material Name
    B. Typical Quantity On Hand
    C. Description of Container
    D. Location
    E. Comments

III. Hazardous Materials Management Procedures and Equipment
    A. Hazardous Materials Storage in Containers
    B. Hazardous Materials Storage in Tanks
    C. Security Systems
    D. Off-Site Shipping of Hazardous Wastes
    E. Inspections/Remedial Actions
    F. Personnel Training

IV. Treatment System(s) Operation
    A. Description of All Treatment Systems and Pollution Control
        Devices
    B. Noting of any Problems

V. Emergency Response
    A. Procedures
    B. Training
    C. Equipment

VI.   Documentation and Recordkeeping
    A.   Review of Required Documents for Completeness and Adequacy
    B.   Noting of any Violations or Problems

VII.   Site Survey
    A.   Key Questions for Interviewing Site Personnel
    B.   Site Inspection
    C.   Facility Inspection/Audit

VIII. Off-Site Transportation and Disposal of Hazardous Waste
    A.   Transporters
    B.   Treatment, Storage and Disposal Facilities

IX.   Special Hazards and Liabilities
    A.   Safety Hazards
    B.   Underground Storage Tanks
    C.   PCBs
    D.   Asbestos
    E.   Radon

X.   Summary of Findings

APPENDIX C

Chemical-Specific ARARs

Selected Chemical-Specific Potential Applicable or Relevant and Appropriate Requirements[a]

Chemical Name	Potential ARARs[b]	
	RCRA Maximum Concentration Limits (mg/l)	SDWA Maximum Contaminant Levels (mg/l)
Arsenic	5.0×10^{-2}	5.0×10^{-2}
Barium	1.0	1.0
Benzene		5.0×10^{-3}
Beta particle photon radioactivity		4 millirems
Cadmium	1.0×10^{-2}	1.0×10^{-2}
Carbon tetrachloride		5.0×10^{-3}
Chromium	5.0×10^{-2}	5.0×10^{-2}
Coliform bacteria		1 per 100 ml
p-Dichlorobenzene		7.5×10^{-2}
1,2-Dichloroethane		5.0×10^{-3}
1,1-Dichloroethylene		7.0×10^{-3}
2-4-Dichlorophenoxyacetic acid (2,4-D)	1.0×10^{-1}	1.0×10^{-1}
Endrin	2.0×10^{-4}	2.0×10^{-4}
Fluoride		4.0
Lead	5.0×10^{-2}	5.0×10^{-2}
Lindane	4.0×10^{-3}	4.0×10^{-3}
Total mercury	2.0×10^{-3}	2.0×10^{-3}
Methoxychlor	1.0×10^{-1}	1.0×10^{-1}
Nitrate (as N)		10
Radionuclides, gross alpha particle activity		15 pCi/l
Radium-226 + radium-228		5 pCi/l
Selenium	1.0×10^{-2}	1.0×10^{-2}
Silver	5.0×10^{-2}	5.0×10^{-2}
Toxaphene	5.0×10^{-3}	5.0×10^{-3}
2,4,5-TP Silvex	1.0×10^{-2}	1.0×10^{-2}
1,1,1-Trichloroethane		2.0×10^{-1}
Trichloroethylene		5.0×10^{-3}
Total trihalomethanes		1.0×10^{-1}
Turbidity		1 Tu
Vinyl chloride		2.0×10^{-3}

Potential ARARs[b]

Chemical Name	CWA Water Quality Criteria for Protection of Human Health		CWA Ambient Water Quality Criteria for Protection of Aquatic Life[c]	
	Water and Fish Ingestion (mg/l)	Fish Consumption Only (mg/l)	Freshwater Acute/Chronic (mg/l)	Marine Acute/Chronic (mg/l)
Acenaphthene			$1.7^*/0.5^*$	$0.9^*/0.7^*$
Acenaphthylene				$3.0 \times 10^{-1*}$
Acrolein	3.2×10^{-1}	7.8×10^{-1}	$6.8 \times 10^{-2*}/2.1 \times 10^{-2*}$	$5.5 \times 10^{-2*}$
Acrylonitrile	5.8×10^{-5}	6.5×10^{-4}	$7.5^*/2.6^*$	
Aldrin	7.4×10^{-8}	7.9×10^{-8}	3.0×10^{-3}	1.3×10^{-3}
Anthracene				
Antimony and compounds	1.5×10^{-1}	45	$9.0/1.6$	
Arsenic and compounds	2.2×10^{-6}	1.8×10^{-5}		
Arsenic (V) and compounds			$0.8^*/4.8 \times 10^{-2*}$	$2.3^*/1.3 \times 10^{-2}$
Arsenic (III) and compounds			$0.3/0.1$	$6.9 \times 10^{-2}/3.6 \times 10^{-2}$
Asbestos	1			
Barium and compounds				
Benz(a)anthracene				
Benz(c)acridine				
Benzene	6.6×10^{-4}	4.0×10^{-2}	5.3^*	
Benzidine	1.2×10^{-4}	5.3×10^{-4}	2.5^*	
Benzo(a)pyrene				
Benzo(b)fluoranthene				
Benzo(ghi)perylene				
Benzo(k)fluoranthene				
Beryllium and compounds	6.8×10^{-6}	1.2×10^{-4}	$0.1^*/5.3 \times 10^{-3*}$	$5.1^*/0.7^*$
Bis(2-chloroethyl)ether				
Bis(2-chloroisopropyl)ether				
Bis(chloromethyl)ether				

Compound				
Cadmium and compounds	1.0×10^{-2}			
Carbon tetrachloride	4.0×10^{-4}	6.9×10^{-3}	$3.9 \times 10^{-3*}/1.1 \times 10^{-3*}$	$4.3 \times 10^{-2}/9.3 \times 10^{-2}$
Chlordane	4.6×10^{-7}	4.8×10^{-7}	3.5×10^{1}	5.0×10^{1}
Chlorinated benzenes			$2.4 \times 10^{-3}/4.3 \times 10^{-6}$	$9.0 \times 10^{-5}/4.0 \times 10^{-6}$
Chlorinated naphthalenes			$2.5 \times 10^{-1*}/5.0 \times 10^{-2*}$	$1.6 \times 10^{-1*}/1.2 \times 10^{-1*}$
Chloroalkyl ethers			$1.6*$	$7.5 \times 10^{-3*}$
Chlorobenzene (mono)			$2.3 \times 10^{2*}$	
Chlorodibromomethane				
Chloroform	1.9×10^{-4}	1.8×10^{-2}		
2-Chlorophenol			$2.8 \times 10^{-1*}/1.2*$	1.0×10^{1}
Chromium III and compounds	170	3433	$4.3*/2.0*$	$1.1/5.0 \times 10^{-2}$
Chromium VI and compounds	5.0×10^{-2}		$1.7*/0.2*$	$2.9 \times 10^{-3}/2.9 \times 10^{-3}$
Copper and compounds			$1.6 \times 10^{2}/1.1 \times 10^{2}$	$1.0 \times 10^{-3}/1.0 \times 10^{-3}$
Cyanides	2×10^{-1}		$1.8 \times 10^{2}/1.2 \times 10^{2*}$	$1.3 \times 10^{-1}/1.0 \times 10^{-6}$
DDT	2.4×10^{-8}	2.4×10^{-8}	$2.2 \times 10^{2}/5.2 \times 10^{3}$	
Dibutyl phthalate	35	154	$1.1 \times 10^{-3}/1.0 \times 10^{-6}$	
Dichlorobenzenes	4×10^{-1}	2.6		
1,2-Dichlorobenzene			$1.1*/7.6 \times 10^{-1*}$	$1.9*$
1,3-Dichlorobenzene				
1,4-Dichlorobenzene				
3,3'-Dichlorobenzidine	1×10^{-4}	2×10^{5}	$1.1 \times 10^{2*}/2.0 \times 10^{1*}$	$1.1 \times 10^{2*}$
1,2-Dichloroethane (EDC)	9.4×10^{-4}	2.4×10^{-1}	$1.1 \times 10^{1*}$	$2.2 \times 10^{2*}$
Dichloroethylenes	3.3×10^{-5}	1.9×10^{-3}	$1.1 \times 10^{1*}$	$2.2 \times 10^{2*}$
1,1-Dichloroethylene	3.1		$2.0*/0.3*$	
2,4-Dichlorophenol				
2,6-Dichlorophenol				
3,4-Dichlorophenol				
2,3-Dichlorophenol				
2,5-Dichlorophenol				
2,4-Dichlorophenoxyacetic acid (2,4-D)	8.7×10^{-2}	14.1	$6.0*/0.2*$	
1,3-Dichloropropene				$0.7*$

Potential ARARs[b]

Chemical Name	CWA Water Quality Criteria for Protection of Human Health		CWA Ambient Water Quality Criteria for Protection of Aquatic Life[c]	
	Water and Fish Ingestion (mg/l)	Fish Consumption Only (mg/l)	Freshwater Acute/Chronic (mg/l)	Marine Acute/Chronic (mg/l)
Dieldrin	7.1×10^{-8}	7.6×10^{-8}	$2.5 \times 10^{-3}/1.9 \times 10^{-6}$	$0.7 \times 10^{-3}/1.9 \times 10^{-6}$
Diethylphthalate	350	1800		
Bis(2-ethylhexyl)phthalate (DEHP)				
Diethylnitrosamine				
7,12-Dimethylbenz(a)anthracene				
Dimethylnitrosamine				
2,4-Dimethylphenol				
Dimethylphthalate	313	2900	2.1^*	
4,6-Dinitro-o-cresol				
2,4-Dinitrophenol				
1,2-Diphenylhydrazine				
Endosulfan	7.4×10^{-2}	1.6×10^{-1}	$2.2 \times 10^{-4}/5.6 \times 10^{-5}$	$3.4 \times 10^{-5}/8.7 \times 10^{-6}$
Endrin	1×10^{-3}		$1.8 \times 10^{-4}/2.3 \times 10^{-6}$	$3.7 \times 10^{-5}/2.3 \times 10^{-6}$
Ethylbenzene	1.4	3.3	3.2×10^{1}	$4.3 \times 10^{-1*}$
Fluoranthene	4.2×10^{-2}	5.4×10^{-2}	3.9^*	$4.0 \times 10^{-2*}/1.6 \times 10^{-2*}$
Fluorides		4.0		
Heptachlor	2.8×10^{-7}	2.9×10^{-7}	$5.2 \times 10^{-4}/3.8 \times 10^{-6}$	$5.3 \times 10^{-5}/3.6 \times 10^{-6}$
Hexachlorobenzene	7.2×10^{-7}	7.4×10^{-7}		
Hexachlorobutadiene	4.5×10^{-4}	5×10^{2}	$9.0 \times 10^{-2}/9.3 \times 10^{-3*}$	$3.2 \times 10^{-2*}$
α-Hexachlorocyclohexane (HCCH)	9.2×10^{-6}	3.1×10^{-5}		
γ-HCCH (Lindane)				
Technical-HCCH	1.2×10^{-5}	4.1×10^{-5}		
Hexachlorocyclopentadiene	2.1×10^{-1}		$7.0 \times 10^{-3*}/5.2 \times 10^{-3*}$	$7.0 \times 10^{-3*}$
Hexachloroethane	1.9×10^{-3}	8.74×10^{-3}	$9.8 \times 10^{-1*}/5.4 \times 10^{-1*}$	$9.4 \times 10^{-1*}$

Compound				
Iodomethane			1.17×10^2*	1.2×10^1*
Isophorone	5×10^2		$8.0 \times 10^{-2}/3.2 \times 10^{-3}$*	$0.1/5.6 \times 10^{-3}$
Lead and compounds (inorganic)	1.4×10^{-4}		$2.4 \times 10^{-3}/1.2 \times 10^{-5}$	$2.14 \times 10^{-3}/2.5 \times 10^{-5}$
Mercury and compounds (alkyl)	1×10^{-1}			
Mercury and compounds (inorganic)			$2.4 \times 10^{-3}/1.2 \times 10^{-5}$	$2.1 \times 10^{-3}/2.5 \times 10^{-5}$
Methoxychlor		1.5×10^{-4}	0.3×10^{-4}*	0.3×10^{-4}*
Methyl chloride				
2-Methyl-4-chlorophenol				
3-Methyl-4-chlorophenol				
3-Methyl-6-chlorophenol				
3-Monochlorophenol				
4-Monochlorophenol				
Nickel and compounds	1.3×10^{-1}		$1.4/1.6 \times 10^{-1}$*	$7.5 \times 10^2/8.3 \times 10^{-3}$
Nitrate (as N)	10			
Nitrobenzene	20		2.7×10^1*	6.6
Nitrophenols			$2.3 \times 10^{-1}/1.5 \times 10^{-1}$*	4.8*
Nitrosamines			5.8*	3.3×10^3*
n-Nitrosodiphenylamine	4.9×10^{-3}	1.6×10^{-2}		
N-Nitrosopyrrolidine	1.6×10^{-5}	9.2×10^{-2}		
Para dichlorobenzene		8.5×10^{-2}		
Pentachlorinated ethanes			7.2*/1.1*	3.9×10^{-1}*/2.8×10^{-1}*
Pentachlorobenzene	7.4×10^{-2}		$2.0 \times 10^2/1.3 \times 10^{-2}$	$1.3 \times 10^2/7.9 \times 10^{-3}$
Pentachlorophenol	1			
Phenanthrene				
Phenol	3.5		$1.0 \times 10^1/2.5$	5.8
Phthalate esters			9.4×10^{-1}*/3.0×10^{-3}*	2.9*/3.4×10^{-3}*
Polychlorinated biphenyls (PCBs)	7.9×10^{-8}		$2.0 \times 10^3/1.4 \times 10^{-5}$	$1.0 \times 10^2/3.0 \times 10^{-5}$
Radionuclides, gross alpha activity		15 pCi/l		
Radium-226 and radium-228		5 pCi/l		
Selenium and compounds	1.0×10^2		$2.6 \times 10^{-1}/3.5 \times 10^{-2}$	$4.1 \times 10^{-1}/5.4 \times 10^2$
Silver and compounds	5.0×10^2		$4.1 \times 10^{-3}/1.2 \times 10^{-4}$	2.3×10^{-3}

Potential ARARs[b]

Chemical Name	CWA Water Quality Criteria for Protection of Human Health		CWA Ambient Water Quality Criteria for Protection of Aquatic Life[c]	
	Water and Fish Ingestion (mg/l)	Fish Consumption Only (mg/l)	Freshwater Acute/Chronic (mg/l)	Marine Acute/Chronic (mg/l)
Strontium-90	8 pCi/l			
2,3,7,8-TCDD (dioxin)			<1.0 × 10^{-5}*/<1.0 × 10^{-8}	
Tetrachlorinated ethanes			9.3*	
1,2,4,5-Tetrachlorobenzene	3.8 × 10^{-2}	4.8 × 10^{-2}		
1,1,2,2-Tetrachloroethane	1.7 × 10^{-4}	1.1 × 10^{-2}	2.4*	9.0*
Tetrachloroethanes			9.3*	
Tetrachloroethylene	8 × 10^{-4}	8.9 × 10^{-3}	5.2*/8.4 × 10^{-1}*	1.0 × 10^{1}*/4.5 × 10^{-1}*
2,3,4,6-Tetrachlorophenol				4.4 × 10^{-1}
Thallium and compounds	1.3 × 10^{-2}	4.8 × 10^{-2}	1.4*/4.0 × 10^{-2}*	2.1 × 10^{-3}*
Toluene	14	420	1.7 × 10^{1}*	6.3*/5.0*
Toxaphene	7.1 × 10^{-7}	7.3 × 10^{-7}	7.3 × 10^{-4}/2.0 × 10^{-7}	2.1 × 10^{-4}/2 × 10^{-7}
Tribromomethane (bromoform)				
Trichlorinated ethanes			1.8 × 10^{1}*	
1,1,1-Trichloroethane	18	1000		3.1 × 10^{1}*
1,1,2-Trichloroethane	6 × 10^{-4}	4.2 × 10^{-2}	9.4*	
Trichloroethylene	2.7 × 10^{-3}	8.1 × 10^{-2}	4.5 × 10^{1}*/2.1 × 10^{1}*	2.0*
Trichloromonofluoromethane				
2,4,5-Trichlorophenol	2.8			
2,4,6-Trichlorophenol	1.2 × 10^{-3}	3.6 × 10^{-3}	9.7 × 10^{-1}*	
2,4,5-Trichlorophenoxypropionic acid				
Trihalomethanes (total)				
Tritium				
Vinyl chloride	2 × 10^{-3}	5.3 × 10^{-1}		
Zinc and compounds			1.3 × 10^{-1}/1.1 × 10^{-1}	9.6 × 10^{-2}/8.6 × 10^{-2}

[a] Additional chemical-specific requirements will be added (e.g., National Ambient Air Quality Criteria) after analysis of additional statutes.

[b] When two or more values conflict, the lower value generally should be used.

[c] Federal water quality criteria (FWQC) are not legally enforceable standards, but are potentially relevant and appropriate to CERCLA actions. CERCLA §121(d)(2)(B)(i) requires consideration of four factors when determining whether FWQC are relevant and appropriate: (1) the designated or potential use of the surface or groundwater, (2) the environmental media affected, (3) the purposes for which such criteria were developed, and (4) the latest information available.

* Lowest observed effect level.

+ Hardness-dependent criteria (100 mg/l used); refer to specific criteria documents for equations to calculate criteria based on other water hardness values.

Sources: "Superfund Public Health Evaluation Manual," U.S. EPA 540/1-86/060 (OSWER Directive 9285.4-1) (October 1986) and "Quality Criteria for Water 1986," U.S. EPA 440/5-86-001 (May 1986) (51 *Fed. Regist.* 43665). Reprinted from "CERCLA Compliance with Other Laws Manual: Draft Guidance," Office of Emergency and Remedial Response, U.S. Report-540/G-89/006 (August 1988).

Sample Contract Provisions

SAMPLE CONTRACT OF SALE INDEMNIFICATION PROVISIONS

1. Notwithstanding any provision in this Agreement to the contrary, it is expressly understood and agreed that the Buyer does not assume or agree to be responsible for, and Seller hereby agrees to indemnify and hold Buyer harmless from and against, any and all claims, obligations, and liabilities and all costs, expenses, and attorneys' fees incurred, based upon or arising out of any obligation, liability, loss, damage, or expense, of whatever kind or nature, contingent or otherwise, known or unknown, incurred under or imposed by any provision of federal, state, or local law or regulation, or common law, pertaining to health, safety, or environmental protection and arising out of the ownership and/or operation of the property by the Seller or any act or omission by Seller, its employees or representatives prior to the execution of this Agreement. It is further understood and agreed that this subsection is a separate and independent agreement, supported by separate consideration, receipt of which is hereby acknowledged, and that this subsection will survive closing and bind the parties hereto.

2. The parties hereto shall enter into a separate agreement, dated as of the date of closing, in form and substance reasonably satisfactory to Buyer, whereunder Sellers, for themselves and their successors and assigns, agree to indemnify and save harmless Buyer from and against any and all claims, demands, causes of action, and suit or suits of any nature whatsoever arising out of the ownership and/or operation of the Real Property by Sellers (known or unknown, contingent or otherwise).

SAMPLE LEASE INDEMNIFICATION PROVISION

Tenant shall indemnify and save harmless Landlord against and from all costs, expenses, liabilities, losses, damages, suits, fines, penalties, claims, and demands of every kind or nature, including reasonable counsel fees, by or on behalf of any person, party, or governmental authority whomsoever, arising out of any accident, injury, or damage which shall happen in, on, or about the

Demised Premises or appurtenances, and on or under the streets, sidewalks, curbs, or vaults in front of or adjacent thereto, however occurring, and for any matter or thing growing out of the occupation, maintenance, alteration, repair, use, or operation of the Demised Premises, or of any part thereof, and/or the streets, sidewalks, curbs, or vaults adjacent thereto during the term.

SAMPLE RESTRICTIVE COVENANT

The Borrower warrants and represents that it will handle, store, and dispose of any materials on the property which under federal, state, or local law, statute, ordinance, or regulations, or court or administrative order or decree require special handling and collection, storage, treatment, or disposal in accordance with all federal, state, and local regulations.

Index

joint and several, 11, 16, 25, 66, 100
lease, 16
lender, 18—19
scope of, 10—11
statutory defenses to, 25—33
subsequent purchaser, 16
lien, 19, 31, 101
liner, 101
local sewer authority, 67
lump sum contracts, 50

manifest, 13, 73, 101
Maryland Bank and Trust, 18, 71
material safety data sheet, 101
maximum contaminant levels (MCL), 57—59
MCL, see Maximum contaminent levels
Mirabile, 18
Monsanto Co., 16
mortgage, 101
Mottolo, 17

National Contingency Plan (NCP), 11—12, 33, 56, 102
National Pollutant Discharge Elimination System (NPDES), 14, 102
National Priorities List (NPL), 10, 12, 42, 48, 102, 103
NCP, see National Contingency Plan
negligence, 19
negotiation of sales contract, 72—76
NEPACCO, 17
New Jersey Department of Environmental Protection, 19, 60
New Jersey Environmental Cleanup and Responsibility Act, 19
New Jersey trigger levels, 60
New York v. Shore Realty Corp., 16, 26, 71

Northernaire Plating Co., 16
notice letter, 31, 102
NPDES, see National Pollutant Discharge Elimination System
NPL, see National Priorities List
nuisance, 19

Occidental Chemical Corp., 29
Occupational Safety and Health Administration (OSHA), 64, 102, 107
off-site contamination, 66—67
on-site contamination, 63—66
operational requirements, 33
operator, 10—11, 14, 16, 18, 25, 28, 30, 67, 74, 79, 102
OSHA, see Occupational Safety and Health Administration
owner, 3, 10—11, 13—14, 16, 18—19, 25, 28, 30—31, 65—67, 74, 79—80, 102

PCBs, see Polychlorinated biphenyls
PEL, see Permissible exposure limit
permissible exposure limit (PEL), 64
permits, 33, 46
Phase I of site assessment, 39, 42—48
contracting for, 50
cost of, 51
Phase II of site assessment, 40, 46—48
Phase III of site assessment, 40
point source, 102—103
polychlorinated biphenyls (PCBs), 15, 65—66
potentially responsible parties (PRPs), 10, 15, 30, 65—66, 103
POTWs, see publicly owned treatment works
pretreatment regulations, 46